Dynamics of the
African/Afro-American
Connection

Dynamics of the African/ Afro-American Connection

From Dependency to Self-Reliance

Edited by
Adelaide M. Cromwell

Howard University Press
Washington, D.C. 1987

Library of Congress Cataloging-in-Publication Data

Dynamics of the African/Afro-American connection, from dependency to self-reliance.

Includes index.
1. Afro-Americans—Relations with Africans.
2. Africa—Economic conditions—1960–
3. Africa—Civilization—20th century. I. Cromwell, Adelaide M.
E185.625.D96   1987   303.4'826'008996073   87–17224
ISBN 0–88258–172–4

To Edward Wilmot Blyden
and Alexander Crummell,
whose words and deeds
have inspired us.

Contents

Foreword

The University of Liberia is pleased to welcome outstanding representatives from the fields of education, journalism, business, and diplomacy from the five neighboring African countries of Sierra Leone, Senegal, Nigeria, Ivory Coast, and Ghana; from the United States of America; and from our own country, Liberia, to this seminar, the "Dynamics of the African/Afro-American Connection: From Dependency to Self-Reliance." Boston University, the University of Sierra Leone, and the University of Liberia have worked together for a number of months, first to secure the small grant from the Ford Foundation, the principal source of funding which has made possible this important gathering of outstanding Africans and Afro-Americans, and then through a seminar held in 1981 at Boston University, at which outstanding black scholars in the United States and scholars from two other African universities joined together to conceptualize and plan for this seminar.

The stated purposes of the seminar are:

1. To assess the present relationship and develop means of improving future communication between Africans and Afro-Americans, with the multiple effect of enhancing their respective identities.
2. To increase the understanding of the Afro-Americans of the complexities and values of African societies and of Africans of the role and status of Afro-Americans in Amerian society.
3. To make more viable and effective the role of Afro-Americans in U.S./African relations.

For a gathering with these purposes in view, this is a significant time, and we look forward to the ideas which will no doubt be generated.

We are in the throes of a difficult world situation. The world is divided and rapidly growing apart. The North-South dichotomy is a stark reality. Mr. Shidrath S. Ramphal characterized this situation as two worlds, "one world united by material comfort and the other united by a common heritage of suffering" (Shidrath S. Ramphal, "International Co-operation and Development: The Role of the Universities," keynote address at the Conference of Vice Chancellors of Commonwealth Universities, Mona, Jamaica, March 26, 1979). African nationals and black people everywhere fall in the latter category, the plight of which grows constantly worse. Years of discussion of a new international economic order without perceptible favorable results for the South have forced on the poor nations which constitute the South the realization that change for social and economic justice will be achieved mainly as a result of major steps they themselves take. Thus, nations and peoples are searching for ways to assert themselves. In so doing, they must reinforce their identities, strengthen existing meaningful alliances, and forge new alliances, if necessary.

That Liberia is the venue of this seminar and the University of Liberia the host institution is fitting, for in the Liberian nation the complexities as well as the contradictions of the African/Afro-American Connection are reflected, although not always clearly. Liberia is a product of two of the undergirding forces of the Connection: race and oppression. Yet, Liberia's place in the struggle for black ascendancy has often been downplayed and Liberia, in many ways, isolated because colonization, which was responsible for the settlement of Liberia in the 1820s and led to the founding of the Liberian nation, seems to figure less prominently in black history than Emancipation or colonialism. The impact of colonization is evident mainly in Liberia and Sierra Leone; however, colonialism adds a different dimension to the situation in Sierra Leone, binding Sierra Leone closer to other African nations, through a shared colonial experience, than to Liberia. While Liberia and Sierra Leone share common indigenous ties of languages and cultural institutions, this fact hardly emerged in the nineteenth-century literature, and even in the twentieth century, these ties have not been used properly as unifying forces for mutual advancement.

Liberia, like Haiti, gained political independence during the nineteenth century, when the world context was dominated with notions of a superior Western civilization, of the inherent inferiority of Africans and the black race, and of Africa as a dark continent. (Formal recognition of Haiti's independence from France was obtained in 1825; however, the nation's original declaration of independence was made January 1, 1804.) Yet, this fact is often not taken into consideration when assessing the evolvement of the Liberian nation. Moreover, colonization was a removal movement, based in the southern United States of America, which advocated the gradual emancipation of slaves, as opposed to abolition, which was based in the northern United States and demanded immediate emancipation of slaves and rights for Afro-Americans within the United States. This, plus the fact that colonization was dominated by ideas of a Christianizing "civilizing" mission, had a lot to do with the vicissitudes suffered by Liberia, particularly in the nineteenth century but which have also strongly affected the development of the nation in the twentieth century. Whether a black nation should be built on Western ideas or on foundations rooted in African cultural values and institutions was a recurring theme and a major concern of the settlers in nineteenth-century Liberia. The easier choice, given the prevailing circumstances, was the former, but when it is evaluated, as it often is, against the twentieth-century context (which has, since the Atlantic Charter and World War II, been favorable to the self-determination of all nations, small as well as large), the choice of Western values has resulted in misinterpretations which have engendered divisiveness among the Liberian people. Moreover, Liberia's major contributions to the black world, which demonstrated, through the building of a nation, that the black man, if given an opportunity, was capable of refinement and advancement and could thereby become a symbol of hope for the black race during the dark days of the continent and of the black race, have often gone unrecognized.

Studies in anthropology, biology, and other disciplines contributed to changing concepts of the black race and of the African continent during the twentieth century. Meanwhile, the twentieth-century scene was dominated by the struggle of most African nations against colonial domination. These nations were aided in their struggle by the Pan-African movement, the first conference of which was held in London in 1900. For the initial years, the movement was not based on the African continent. The initiatives as well as important leadership roles were played by Africans in the diaspora. The focus was mainly political, and the movement facilitated the building of a network of black leaders and gave impetus to the uniting of black people. In time, the Pan-African movement became an integral part of the life of the African continent.

With the wave of independence on the African continent, particularly between the late 1950s and the early 1970s, a new day dawned. However, political independence and relief from colonial domination for many African countries did not lead, as many expected, to social and economic justice in the global community nor, for that matter, within the African countries. The winds of change, nevertheless, had positive effects upon the struggle by Afro-Americans for equity in education and in the economy and for greater participation in the political life of their country. Moreover, their struggle contributed to the enhancement of the image and dignity of black people. The resulting movement for equality and dignity for Africans, expressed in concepts such as the *African Personality* and *Négritude*, was popularized, and these concepts became foci for identification by blacks everywhere, giving them psychological buttressing, in contrast to much earlier years when, although advocated by a few like Dr. Edward W. Blyden, they were hardly understood or taken seriously.

Meanwhile, in postindependence Africa, nationalism moved to center stage. African leaders, aware of their political power, became anxious about the building of their respective nation-states, which equipped them to assert themselves as such and to assume responsibility for their destinies. The continent became balkanized and, with these developments, a shift in the nature and strength of the Connection occurred.

The impact of the global political-economic system, however, soon drove home the reality that political independence cannot be truly meaningful unless it is buttressed by economic independence. Africa became occupied with trying to establish means of regional cooperation for economic and political strength through various organizations, principal among them the Organization of African Unity (OAU). Although the African nations were preoccupied with the continent, solutions to the continent's problems were elusive. During this same period, Afro-Americans struggled with similar dilemmas.

How, in view of this reality, can the Connection be revitalized?
- It is interesting to note that there are parallels between the various movements in the African/Afro-American Connection: for example, abolition and the integration-nationalist movement, as against colonization and Garveyism. Conflicts between these movements, it seems, have been influenced by education, economic standing, and the social-class background of proponents and followers, somewhat similar to the cleavage in Africa between the educated urban elite and the rural or urban poor, who often are uneducated.

What can be done to mend this cleavage? What insights need to be developed?
- Africans and Afro-Americans are interacting within the global framework based on their paticular situations and strengths at given periods.

Cooperative relations can be made more fruitful if Africans and Afro-Americans enhance their respective strengths. How can this be done?
- The economic dependence of both Africans and Afro-Americans is apparent and is a great handicap to their affecting, on the international scene, that much-talked-about new international economic order.

What can be done to achieve economic independence and strength? Are there untapped resources which can be identified, harnessed, and shared? How can education figure in all of this, particularly in human resource development, so that blacks will have requisite skills, insights, and sensitivities?

- Indeed, social and economic justice in the international community will be achieved only if appropriate steps are taken by those who share the common heritage of suffering.

And now, returning to the task I set out to perform, I do wish each participant, on behalf of us all at the University of Liberia, a hearty welcome. May the intellectual exchanges in this seminar lay foundations to move us nearer to our goal of an equitable world.

Mary Antoinette Brown Sherman
President, University of Liberia
Monrovia, Liberia

Message to
Seminar Participants

On the occasion of the convening of this seminar, under the theme the "Dynamics of the African/Afro-American Connection," it gives me great pleasure, on behalf of the People's Redemption Council and in my own name, to extend to you sincere greetings and best wishes for the success of this historic meeting. It is also our privilege to welcome the many distinguished delegates who have come to Liberia for this occasion and to wish that their stay among us wil be most pleasant and rewarding.

We note with interest that this seminar is designed to examine the extent of African/Afro-American solidarity and to devise means of promoting our common identities. This meeting is expected to create greater understanding of the complexities and values inherent in African norms and traditions as well as of the role and status of the Afro-American in the United States. In addition, your meeting is important to us in Liberia because it affords academics, business leaders, and professionals from a number of African countries and the United States the opportunity to meet here at our national university.

We need not emphasize that you are meeting at a time of great social, cultural, and economic transformations in Liberia. Since our revolution of April 12, 1980, we have endeavored to promote justice and human rights, long denied the majority of our people. We hope that during this seminar you will have the opportunity to understand the dynamics of the present changes in Liberia.

Liberia's historic role as a torch bearer of the cause of the struggling people of Africa and of the diaspora must not be underemphasized. The strengthening of this role becomes a cornerstone of our revolution. We consider it a distinguished privilege to host this seminar because it builds on the historical foundations of the nationalist struggle in Africa. This fight against colonialism and imperialism saw the gathering of Africans from the continent and those in diaspora in six significant Pan-African congresses during the first half of this century. As a result of those congresses, our perspective of ourselves was sharpened, our resolve to fight oppression was strengthened, and our direction became clearer.

Today, results of those Pan-African congresses can be seen in the achievement of independence by nearly all African countries, the gains of the civil rights struggle in the United States, and the emergence of independent nations in the Caribbean.

Because of the great strides made in the last three decades, it is very important that Africans at home, and in the diaspora, continue their consultations to ensure that freedom does not become an empty dream and that independence does not lapse into dependency. We should concentrate our efforts on the protection of our gains in civil rights and statehood. We should perceive ours as being in a continuous struggle until we develop the productive capacities, the distribution mechanisms, and the appropriate value predispositions that would enable us to become masters of our own destinies.

We want to thank the organizers and sponsors of this seminar and to assure you that we look forward with eagerness to the success of your deliberations.

In the cause of the people, the struggle continues!

Samuel K. Doe
Head of State
and Chairman,
the People's Redemption Council
Monrovia, Liberia

Preface

Africans and Afro-Americans through the years have struggled, against tremendous odds, to maintain effective communication with each other—individually and in groups—on the continent of Africa, in Europe, and in the United States. This was most difficult when Afro-Americans were slaves and when Africans vigorously colonized. Yet the tie was never broken.

The twentieth century has been the time for strengthening and accelerating that communication. Years of freedom for Afro-Americans and the stimulus of two world wars fed the desire and offered increasing opportunities for Africans, at home and abroad, to assess their collective condition and to take steps to be mutually supportive.

These endeavors have occurred most frequently within the spheres of politics and culture. The Pan-African movement expressed in the conferences in England, Europe, and the United States; in organizations such as the Society for African Culture in Paris and its U.S. counterparts, the American Society for African Culture, the American Negro Leadership Conference, and the Council on African Affairs; and in cultural celebrations held in Senegal, Nigeria, and Tanzania all testify to the political and cultural basis of the move toward improved international communication.

Academic interest among Africans and Afro-Americans in each other's history and culture usually has been on an individual basis or within the larger context of academia, where both Africans and Afro-Americans not only are outnumbered but also often find the concerns more Euro-centric than Afro-centric. Compared to Africans, Afro-Americans have had, for a much longer time, institutions of higher learning within their own communities, as it were, and have had nominal, if not complete, control over them; however, these universities have not, for the most part, played a significant role in improving the communications between Africans and Afro-Americans.

It is not surprising, however, that the two oldest Sub-Saharan African universities—The University of Liberia and the University of Sierra Leone through Fourah Bay College—would join Boston University, which has the first graduate program in Afro-American studies, to assess the present situation and to develop means of improving communication between Africans and Afro-Americans. Adopting these goals had a dual effect: the two groups' identities were enhanced, making more beneficial and effective the role of Afro-Americans in U.S./African relations; and the understanding of each other's roles and status was improved, thus achieving a more stable world community.

xvii

The presidents of the three universities—Dr. Mary Antoinette Brown Sherman, Dr. Arthur Porter, and Dr. John R. Silber—felt that the university community should serve as the site of workshops, conferences, and other forms of deliberations where scholars and other citizens could pursue and achieve the goals of self-assessment and improved communication. Accordingly, in 1977 a proposal was submitted to the Ford Foundation, which funded a small workshop held at Boston University in April 1981 to clarify the issues, formulate appropriate strategies, and propose an agenda and a format for a seminar to be held in Africa.

Workshop participants agreed to hold the first seminar at the University of Liberia. Dr. Sherman agreed to extend the invitation to the scholars selected from the United States and to the scholars nominated by West African ambassadors in Liberia.

This volume includes a summary interpretation of the initial workshop held at Boston University, followed by the papers presented at the seminar in January 1983 in Liberia and contributions by discussants.

Adelaide M. Cromwell
Boston University
Boston, Massachusetts

Dynamics of the
African/Afro-American
Connection

Key Issues and Changing Dynamics of the African/Afro-American Connection: A Summary Interpretation of the Boston University Planning Workshop

Pearl T. Robinson

HOWEVER significant the historical ties between Africans and Afro-Americans, the problems of the 1980s call for new kinds of strategic relationships. Such links can best be forged by the joint exploration of issues and alternatives. Thus, while Afro-Americans search for appropriate ways to relate to a changing Africa, Africans would do well to learn more about factors—past and present—which shape the lives of black Americans. With these considerations in mind, Boston University's Afro-American Studies Program, the University of Liberia, and the University of Sierra Leone cosponsored a forum to discuss ways of strengthening the African/Afro-American Connection.[1]

Historically, the Pan-African movement was both a symbol and a strategy for consolidating greater unity among black people. Its goals included national independence for colonial subjects and equal citizenship rights for Afro-Americans. That initial phase accomplished a lot, but it has now played itself out. As the twentieth century draws to a close, transnational alliances based on race are floundering for want of a strong rationale.[2] In times such as these, effective collaboration

3

between Africans and Afro-Americans will require greater clarity of purpose.

What kinds of relationships are possible in the current geopolitical setting? How vital are the areas of common interest to the everyday concerns of blacks in each sphere? Will ideological constraints and centrifugal forces prevent the consolidation of Pan-African political alliances? Answers to these and related questions should help to chart a steady course. The present situation poses a challenge—a challenge to understand the new realities and to use them as a basis for forging ahead.

Education

A fundamental impasse to viable alliance strategies is the knowledge gap which separates peoples of African descent. Although the problem is most serious across continental divides, African national boundaries are also implicated. The knowledge gap results from educational systems that are Euro-centric, inward-looking, or parochial in concept. In colonial times, the African's access to information about Afro-Americans was circumscribed. Today, Afro-American scholars complain that it is increasingly difficult to know what African intellectuals are producing.[3] Thus, in the absence of concerted efforts, the gap will likely widen.

The requisite educational reforms have been slow to materialize, but would-be innovators can turn to some notable experiments of proven success. These are programs that promote an Afro-centric perspective and build on comparative studies of the black experience. They exist in a few African locales and provide the premise for black studies at certain American universities. One African-based example is the University of Nairobi's comparative literature curriculum, which uses material cultural analysis as its principal methodology. Students are taken through a three-phased process. They begin by studying the oral traditions of Africa, black America, and the West Indies as well as symbolic cultural objects from each of those areas. Next they move on to the literature of other colonized peoples. Only after this grounding in Third World perspectives do they go on to study European literature.[4] The approach clearly has validity for fields other than literature, but there are too few opportunities for academics to know what is going on across disciplines, let alone in other parts of the world.

This brings us to an important and often overlooked aspect of educational reform: communications. African and Afro-American educational planners must begin to accord higher priority to the techniques and technology of accessing information. Otherwise, teachers and researchers who are separated by great distances will spend inordinate amounts of time reinventing the wheel. There is a role here for persons with a special kind of expertise—engineers of education. These would be people with the requisite technical skills to match a particular problem with the appropriate information and problem-solvers.[5] For those concerned with creating a body of comparative Pan-African scholarship, the education engineer's skills would be useful at every phase of the process—from research to publication to dissemination of materials.

The need for this technical input serves notice that the African/Afro-American Connection will not be able to flourish if it is restricted to occasional face-to-face contacts and communications via the written word. The educational medium of the future is electronics, although in the short run it may be too expensive for blacks to control. Film has long been an excellent means of cross-cultural education, and its relative cost is much more manageable. The *Faces of Change* film series is a good model.[6] This collection contains five films apiece about five different cultures—twenty-five films in all. In each set of five there is one film that presents an overview of the culture, another that shows the process of education, and so on. More such films on the various African cultures should be produced. It would be equally valuable for Africans to have comparable films about Afro-Americans.

With innovative applications of the communications media and modest resources carefully targeted, we can begin closing the knowledge gap. The present abyss points to the importance of developing relationships between Africanist academics and blacks with the technical skills required to implement these ideas. It also points to the collaborative endeavors between African and Afro-American universities needed to facilitate the consolidation of institutional ties. As heirs to a worldwide tradition of literate blacks who have contributed their talents to the struggle for racial progress, today's black intellectuals should have the wherewithal to reach beyond the walls of the ivory tower.

Leadership

Let us now consider whether the transnational leadership ties exist to spearhead viable and effective alliance strategies between Africans and Afro-Americans. To put the issue into perspective, it is useful to recall the nature of the leadership network that spawned the anticolonial nationalist movement. In contrast to the current diffuse black leadership, prior to independence the leadership network was easily discernible.[7] Missionary groups and churches were very important arenas; they fostered relationships through education. Prominent personalities in black institutions of higher learning were key actors, including college presidents, educators, and student leaders. Individuals in the U.S. civil rights organizations, particularly the NAACP and the Urban League, were pivotal. And people on a variety of cultural levels—from Paul Robeson to black sailors who brought news to Calabar to the African students and teachers returning from abroad—provided critical supportive linkages.

Even in the contemporary period, we find that most of the political leaders in Africa and the West Indies have a Pan-African connection. For many, these ties were formed while they were being educated in the colonial metropole or during the course of the various Pan-African conferences. Among the younger generation of military rulers, more obscure links are now beginning to surface. Liberia's Samuel Doe, for instance, spent several years at a Garveyite technical school in Monrovia.[8]

Contact void of content, however, has little practical consequences. Conceptually, we need to establish the purposes and situate the boundaries in time and space of black leadership ties. Placing these relationships in historical context is necessary because achievement of the political and constitutional goals of the nationalist and civil rights movements transformed the nature of personal and institutional interaction. Today, in order to talk analytically about black leaders, we must make clear distinctions among those who have positions of authority in a variety of nongovernmental organizations, those who hold formal political power in any of a number of locales in the state system, and those who function in international agencies. Finally, we need to delineate precisely transactional fields in order to sort gratuitous encounters from purposeful linkages.

Two issue areas critically important to the well-being of black communities in Africa and in the diaspora are economic development and U.S. military policies. Both are susceptible to U.S. domestic political lobbying, and both have a foreign policy component. Although former UN Ambassador Andrew Young made linkage between increased trade with Africa and job creation for urban black Americans the centerpiece of his vision as mayor of Atlanta, in general there has been far too little Pan-African collaboration around economic development issues. And despite the establishment in 1978 of TransAfrica, a black political lobby for Africa and the Caribbean, Afro-Americans have had no significant influence on U.S. military involvement in Africa.

This regrettable situation is the result of a lapse in leadership. The time has come for more creative thinking about collaborative strategies to harness the economic potential of the black world. Through such efforts, aid for economic and social development could become multi-directional, linking private- as well as public-sector ventures originating in the United States, the Caribbean, or Africa. Similarly, expanded transnational consultations among blacks with international expertise would upgrade the input of Afro-Americans in foreign-policy lobbying. Finally, greater cultivation of cross-professional ties among blacks who share an interest in a particular issue area such as food policy might encourage those in the foundation world, aid agencies, agricultural research institutes, and business to put their heads together and devise new ways to deal with some intractable problems.

There is nothing to suggest that African governments will take the lead in promoting initiatives along these lines. Indeed, in some cases the governments are themselves part of the problem. Yet, all avenues must be explored when considering the crucial matter of funding. Today's Pan-African leadership networks may be too fragile to thrive without state support, but their effectiveness will depend upon flexibility, a degree of autonomy, and the capacity to carry on while challenging the status quo.

Global System

To gain a perspective on the environmental factors that affect the possibilities for establishing linkages, relations between Africans and Afro-Americans can be examined in terms of systems analysis. The concept of a global system[9] with political, economic, and cultural dimensions that vary over time situates the evolution of the Connection in a larger process of international change.

Numerous factors are operating to transform the global system. In the aftermath of decolonization, alterations in the patterns of political relationships redefined what actors could do. Beginning in Europe, the centrality of the nation-state has been eroding and giving way to regionalism. Satellite technology has compressed the global system by reducing the constraints of geographical boundaries. As a result, today's world is characterized by the penetration and interdependence of domestic and international spheres. Relations among the states, international organizations, multinational corporations (MNCs), as well as subnational actors all have to be taken into account.

Given these global dynamics, the question is whether Pan-Africanism can provide practical solutions to problems. Only time will tell because at present the indicators are equivocal. In the positive vein, there are now a number of identifiable ethnic blocs active in international politics, and current trends suggest that a new "transism"[10] based on race, religion, ideology, and affluence is correlated with demands for global reform. The Geneva Group of ten Western countries and Japan, the Latin Americans, the Arabs, and the Africans have been major protagonists in debates over international democratization and equity. Issues raised include trade policies such as special preferences and commodity agreements, transfer of technology, a code of conduct for MNCs, and demands for greater equality in the decision-making authority of international economic institutions.

In some respects, the global system has already been modified by trilateral allocations of power. The divisions represented in the elusive new international economic order (NIEO) negotiations are the European Economic Community (EEC), the United States, and the Group of 77 (G-77) standing for the Third World bloc.[11] In a more concrete example, votes in the International Fund for Agriculture and Development (IFAD) are allocated equally among the West, the G-77, and OPEC. The fact that the United States is the only state actor functioning unilaterally in the NIEO discussions highlights its special position in this emerging trilateral system. But the input of Afro-Americans, who do not have a government to support their particular interests as blacks, varies with the politics of the incumbent U.S. president and with their ability to influence that president's policies.

This state of affairs points to the limitations of reforms that focus on inequities at the international level without addressing the internal and external relationships of blacks within the global system. In many instances, transnational class alliances that link economic elites across race are much more vigorous than Pan-African ties—even when the consequences impair African economic development. Therefore, the fact that the Third World is now calling for a new North-South order should not be taken a priori as an indication that things are changing. Since the new trilateralism excludes the planned economies, concessions won in international forums are not shielded from the consequences of East-West strategic competition. Moreover, just as the U.S. civil rights revolution has proved inconsequential for the economic predicament of a growing black underclass, there is no guarantee that NIEO will better the lot of Africa's rural or urban poor.

What can be asserted at this point is that a greater potential for change exists now than at any period since the burgeoning of the nationalist movement in the 1950s. But opportunity can only be transformed into positive action by the deeds of determined women and men. Because power relations in the global system are mediated through capital, Africans and Afro-Americans need to concentrate on the development of their own domestic, internally controlled economic resources. This is a task most amenable to a bottom-up approach whereby individuals or institutions based in local black communities have greater leeway to foster self-reliance and to promote social relations free of racial discrimination and class exploitation. The proliferation of such internal changes in strategic locales throughout the global system would eventually strengthen the hand of African delegations in international forums—enabling them to do more than simply block other states' initiatives or ask for higher prices for coffee. And in such an environment, the collaborative ventures between Africans and Afro-Americans so essential to a Pan-African strategy of accumulation would be far more lucrative and beneficial.

Cultural Identity

Much of the preceding discussion carries the implicit assumption that race and shared origin provide a sound foundation for collaborative behavior. But does it necessarily follow that these roots engender a common cultural identity that can be mobilized in the black struggle for liberation and equality? No. The two propositions are related but quite distinct. Just how relevant is cultural kinship to the African/Afro-American Connection? To answer this question, we must first define *culture.*

For purposes of this analysis, *culture* denotes how people relate to their material environment in order to define themselves as a social entity. It is necessary to make a distinction between material culture (objects created, food, shelter, clothing) and nonmaterial culture. Black people in different locales may not share the same material culture, but a contextual definition of *culture* reveals the basis of black kinship.[12] The key contextual elements of black cultural identity are (1) the commonality of a historical experience that links African origins, trans-Atlantic slavery, and political denial; (2) the combination of economic barriers and exploitation based on race; and (3) similar environmental factors that replicate patterns of structural inferiority. More than simply a shared experience of oppression, however, the emphasis here is on cultural resiliency and the affective bond between Africans and blacks in the diaspora.

Now we can return to the question of whether mobilization on the basis of cultural kinship has any practical significance in a world where so much of what really matters revolves around money and power.[13] Historically, we find that the tendency for black intellectuals and activists to focus on culture is associated with two strikingly different attitudes or tactics: political retrenchment on the one hand and mass mobilization on the other. In the case of Afro-Americans, culture has served as a refuge from politics during periods of repression such as the crackdown on the Left in the late 1920s and McCarthyism in the 1950s. Yet, cultural nationalism was the motive force that propelled the mass-mobilization tactics of economic Garveyism in the early 1920s as well as the black power political awakening of the 1960s. This polarity attests to the malleability of culture as a medium of social discourse. In effect, it can function as both an instrument for power and a refuge from weakness.

The point to be emphasized is that the celebration of black ethnicity can be a very effective means of mobilization and recruitment to the cause of Pan-African renewal—in the established tradition of religious revivalism. But to move beyond catharsis, those who celebrate black ethnicity have to become practitioners of the mundane requisites of economic and political consolidation. Since this change is neither easy nor automatic, the outcome depends on leadership choices. To the extent that black cultural identity is embedded in a context of denial in the global system, African and Afro-American leaders will need to rely on a diversified arsenal as they wage a protracted struggle on multiple fronts.

Economics

Contemporary Pan-Africanists in search of a Promethean challenge need not look beyond the realm of economics. The mid-1970s crisis of international capitalism brought in its wake world recession, structural changes in Western economies, and a persistent fall in the demand and prices for Africa's export commodities. Despite the apparition of recovery in the advanced industrial economies, the black condition has suffered new setbacks. Afro-Americans are feeling the impact of shifts in the allocations of public and private resources as a result of changes in U.S. industrial policy. Africans, for their part, face far more dire prospects.

In the view of Adebayo Adedeji, executive secretary of the Economic Commission for Africa (ECA), five potentially devastating crises threaten the continent with economic collapse and consequent social and political disaster. These are the food crisis, the energy crisis, an escalating deterioration in the terms of trade, a balance-of-payments crisis with related debt servicing problems, and a crisis of economic management. If relations between Africans and Afro-Americans continue to eschew these critical issue areas, the import of a sense of shared cultural identity will inevitably decrease in salience. The dynamics of Pan-Africanism have changed, and the educational outreach of intellectuals combined with the communication capabilities via film, computer, and satellite technology are needed to help bring this new reality into focus.

The current range of economic problems on the continent is exceedingly broad. Moreover, by most accounts, African economies show few signs of improving before the end of this century. Projections done for the World Bank, the ECA, and the UN paint a picture of deterioration and continued decline.[14] But the doomsayers have not precipitated withdrawal from Africa. To the contrary, bilateral and multilateral aid-donor agencies have redoubled their efforts to formulate new agendas for action, to identify untapped investment opportunities, to reorder the postindependence priorities of African governments, and to bring about economic policy adjustments. A good deal of this activity is at the sufferance of African governments that have had to toe the line in order to get the financial assistance they covet. And to an extent far greater than ever before, the U.S. Agency for International Development is playing a leading role in these economic policy dialogues.

In the midst of these operations to salvage African economies, careers are being built: people with the relevant technical skills and expertise are expanding their networks and cementing linkages that will last a professional lifetime. Particularly because so much of what is being proposed is controversial or contrary to the notion of self-reliance, the time is ripe for new thinking about ways to strengthen the African/Afro-American Connection. Relationships that revolve around economic development strategies ought to be in the vanguard.

Of course, it is one thing to proclaim the merits of transnational collaboration among blacks who share a concern for Africa's economic future but quite another to bring such partnerships into being. One natural incubation site ought to be the university. Many African and West Indian students go to the United States for advanced technical training and have opportunities to develop close personal ties in the Afro-American community. But today we find that these groups are not gravitating toward each other around economic goals the way their predecessors two generations ago did around political goals. One explanation for this new pattern is related to the transformation of the global system. Over the past several decades there have been dramatic structural changes in the job market facing highly trained African students. Before independence, their sights were fixed on top-level civil service jobs, but to get those jobs they had to first gain control of the state. Today, however, the most attractive positions are with the MNCs, and employment does not depend on control of the economy. Thus, the personal professional motivation that compelled African students to cultivate political alliances with Afro-American students has dissipated and has yet to be replaced by a more compelling economic rationale.

Entrepreneurs and risk takers will probably be the organizers of most collaborative schemes that materialize in the current situation. Success will depend upon the right combination of technical skills, management expertise, and strategic connections. For those Africans or Afro-Americans willing to leave the security of the corporate structure after a period of apprenticeship, the requisite entrées and networks should pose less of a problem. However, the choices of what to do and where to intervene are determinant and therefore require the utmost scrutiny.

In addition to collaboration on policy-planning activities, there is a role for business ventures. Creative use of "set-asides" by African and Caribbean governments could open up new opportunities for Afro-American companies to gain Third World experience and improve their competitive edge. Middle-level African institutions such as the African Development Bank could do more to enable African entrepreneurs and parastatals to secure contract work for projects they fund. Black-owned, joint-venture companies ought to be encouraged. This sort of overture could do much to boost the capabilities of African and Afro-American firms in the lucrative market of basic infrastructure, rural development, and related services.

Now the critical question is whether earnings—whatever their source—will be transferred to socially useful activities. While the profit motive is perforce a predominant element in business undertakings, normative considerations are likewise important if one is concerned with the long-term prospects for Africa. Should the forecasters prove correct, all of these propositions may be little more than short-run palliatives. Nevertheless, if a new breed of economic institutions can foster a bit more local control and point the way toward equitable use of the economic surplus, then there will be something on which to build when Africa does emerge from its present economic morass.

Politics

We have considered a variety of fronts along which blacks can join forces across national boundaries in mutually beneficial endeavors. The viability of these ideas is ultimately a matter of political will. Policies and personal linkages are pivotal. Still, it is important to be especially meticulous in the political arena because relations in this domain pose the greatest constraints.

To understand the nuances that make some forms of cooperation more difficult than others, an appreciation of the different political contexts in which blacks function is essential.[15] Power and purpose are two key variables. Whereas Africans and Afro-Caribbeans now have political control in the state system, Afro-Americans have sought political participation within the state. Africans preside over black majoritarian societies that harbor no economically marginalized, despised racial minorities. The West Indies are also black majoritarian societies, but pluralistic communities reduce the dimensions of that majority. Afro-Americans, however, live in black minoritarian societies and do not set the norms of racial articulation within the U.S. polity. Race-conscious political actors in these three contexts have differing abilities to use the state for their purposes. Moreover, inasmuch as states express themselves in terms of ideology or national interests, racial solidarity may be at odds with either or both of these frames of reference.

Revolutionary Marxism and Islam are two examples of political ideologies that preempt claims to the primacy of race. At times, the virulence of class conflict within racial or ethnic boundaries may exceed that of confrontation between the groups. Likewise, race and nationality are incidental to political Islam's definition of the *Ulema* or community of the faithful. Efforts to consolidate cooperative ventures among blacks in the face of such prior political commitments may well languish for lack of a constituency.

This litany of constraints notwithstanding, there still remains considerable political space within which to maneuver. At the subnational level in particular, black intellectuals, technocrats, and public officials from various locales in the global system frequently interact in informal settings around matters that have policy implications. At the level of national politics, states often adjust their policies in response to pressure, and much more could be done in this regard. Afro-Americans, for example, have yet to master the well-established tradition of ethnicity in U.S. foreign policy whereby "hyphenated" Americans lobby to channel national resources and shape policies to favor their homelands. Finally, at the level of international relations there are certain structural positions of power—ranging from chair of the Africa Subcommittee in the U.S. House of Representatives to director of the World Bank—which carry policy prerogatives, prior access to information, and a privileged role in the allocation of resources. Though occasionally held by blacks, such strategic placements have been underused in the cause of trans-Africanism, or a coming together politically.

As the forces of the twentieth century transform the dynamics of global exchange, the African/Afro-American Connection stands poised at the dusk of dawn. Postcolonial issues, emerging technologies, and mobilization strategies will determine the tide of the future. The early Pan-Africanists continue to serve as models of perceptivity and determination, but the current task requires the ability to discern new horizons.

NOTES

1. A workshop was held April 20–23, 1981, at Boston University. It was followed by a seminar in Monrovia hosted by the University of Liberia January 10–15, 1983. This essay is based on the workshop proceedings. See Appendix C for a complete list of workshop participants.
2. The recurring problems of the Organization of African Unity and the Arab League as well as the more recent difficulties facing the European Economic Community underscore the fact that viable international alliances require a rationale other than race.
3. This problem of communications between African and Afro-American scholars was raised at the seminar in Boston.
4. Micere M. Githae Mugo, former Dean of the Faculty of Arts at the University of Nairobi, presented a summary of this curriculum innovation at the seminar.
5. The notion of developing a new profession of specialists who would be engineers of education was proposed by Willard Johnson, a professor of political science at the Massachusetts Institute of Technology.
6. These suggestions for expanding the educational uses of film were offered by anthropologist James Gibbs, Jr., of Stanford University.
7. E. U. Essien-Udom of the University of Ibadan's political science department provided this characterization of the black anticolonial leadership network.
8. Historian Tony Martin of Wellesley College traced Doe's Garvey connection.
9. The *global system* concept was introduced into the seminar discussion by anthropologist Elliott Skinner of Columbia University.
10. The term *transism* was introduced by Herschelle Challenor of UNESCO. Much of the discussion which follows is based on Challenor's elaboration of *transism*.
11. The G–77, which now numbers over 100, includes the African, Latin American, and Asian countries in the Third World bloc.
12. Micere Mugo provided this contextual definition of *culture*.
13. This question was raised by historian Nathaniel Huggins of Harvard University, who offered the view that culture is a refuge of weakness.
14. See The World Bank, *World Development Report 1982* (New York: Oxford University Press, 1982); Economic Commission for Africa, "ECA and Africa's Development, 1983–2008—A Preliminary Perspective Study" (Addis Ababa, 1983); and the UN commissioned study by Wassily Leontif, et al. (New York: Oxford University Press, 1977), *inter alia, The Future of the World Economy: A United Nations Study.* Willard Johnson's paper in this volume examines the Leontif study in some detail.
15. This typology of the black political context was contributed by Herschelle Challenor.

Personal Networks and Institutional Linkages in the Global System

Elliott P. Skinner

THE necessity of African peoples to deal with difficult and sometimes similar problems resulting from their contact with Europeans stimulated the development of personal networks and institutional linkages among them. Like other human groups, African peoples have had to adapt to various ecologies and local historical circumstances. In the process, their sociocultural systems, languages, and even their physical types have changed. Yet, so pervasive were the characteristics of the emerging European-controlled global system which progressively enveloped them, that far-flung African and African-derived peoples often found common ground for social action. Moreover, the types of networks and institutions, and the fate of these entitites, reflected the major transformations in the history of this global system.[1]

For purposes of analysis, it may be helpful to consider the history of these networks and institutional linkages as falling into four major phases. The first period started with the "Age of Discovery," extended through the height of the slave trade, accompanied the rise of capitalism, and terminated with revolts among both blacks and whites against slavery and domination by Europeans. The "abolitionist period," the second phase, was characterized by the drive to end slavery, to repatriate Africans in Sierra Leone and Liberia, and by the efforts of the early black educators, missionaries and diplomats, to defend what was called the "black nationality." This phase ended with the partititioning of the African continent. The third period, the "Pan-African phase," starting with the dawn of the twentieth century, was

15

characterized by increasing contacts among African peoples (facilitated by labor migrations and urbanization), major regional wars and World Wars, and the rise of socialism and ended with the beginning of the decolonization process. The "contemporary period," the fourth phase, is characterized by the proliferation of sovereign nation-states in Africa and among African-derived populations in the Caribbean; the cold war conflict between capitalist and socialist states and its impact on African peoples; the issues of race and class among peoples; and the rising demands of formerly colonized and dependent peoples for a major restructuring of the global system by means of a new international economic order and a new international communications order. For reasons of both time and space this essay treats only aspects of phases one and two, paying special attention to the activities of the early black diplomats in Liberia.

Europeans bent on conquering, Christianizing, and exploiting the world first encountered those black Africans living at the periphery of the great inland Sudanese states and empires. Innocent of the latent power of the Europeans, the Africans had no complexes due to race and so demanded and received respect from their visitors. Yet, there were signs of things to come. Quite early in the encounter, Europeans seized Africans and transported them to Europe to be enslaved and Christianized. Other Africans were taken to Europe either as hostages or with the consent of their people for education and conversion to Christianity. Some of these Africans, such as Philip Quaque of the Gold Coast and Price Aniaba of Assini in the Ivory Coast, while surprised by the nature of European civilization, gave good accounts of themselves and their people.[2] On the other hand, a number of returnees served as agents for a Europe now becoming increasingly arrogant as its soldiers and traders gained the upper hand in their relations with the West and Central Africans. In South Africa, small groups of European settlers pushed aside or enclaved the populations, and in East Africa, the Portuguese conquered the littoral and increased the centuries-long slave trade. The rape of Africa and its peoples had started, but the Europeans were now more interested in developing the New World as plantations and as places for settlement than in penetrating into the heart of Africa.[3]

It did not take the Europeans long to discover that they could not develop their newly found lands without African labor. The Spaniards started this tradition by transporting their Christianized blacks, called *ladinos* (in contrast to non-Christianized blacks called *bozals*), because although they needed labor they did not want any infidels in their new realms. However, almost immediately the Africans transported for labor started a tradition of networking to defend and to protect themselves. In 1522, twenty Africans working on the sugar mill of Admiral Diego Columbus united with others who spoke the same language and fled the plantation, killing Spaniards in the process. Throughout New Spain, New France, Brazil, Surinam, the Caribbean, and the North American continent, Africans used whatever cultural and linguistic traits they had in common, or could create, to oppose their enslavement.[4] The number of shipboard revolts among slaves being transported to the New World amply testifies to the speed with which Africans from various regions could and did unite to defend themselves in the face of a common dilemma. Moreover, the Africans took every opportunity during the European Wars of Empire in the New World and in the so-called Age of Revolution to agitate and struggle for their freedom.[5]

Among the most vocal of those blacks opposed to slavery in the New World were the articulate freed persons in British North America. Moreover, these early blacks were quite prepared to return to Africa. One group in Massachusetts petitioned the British governor in 1773 in the following words: "We are willing to submit to such regulations and laws, as may be made relative to us, until we leave the province, which we are determined to do as soon as we can, from our joint labours, procure money to transport ourselves to some part of the Coast of *Africa*, where we propose a settlement."[6] The British refused this request, and a black man, Crispus Attucks, was one of the first "rebels" to die in the American revolution. Other blacks did join the British who promised them freedom. Some of these would later go to Nova Scotia and subsequently move to Sierra Leone, where they became the nucleus of a black educated network for all of West Africa. Those blacks who fought for the "rebels" found to their dismay that the emerging United States of America was not prepared to grant them either freedom or equality. They had to struggle for it.[7]

Recognizing quite early that they had to build institutions to gain freedom, blacks in the New World began to mobilize. In 1775 Prince Hall, who had immigrated to Massachusetts from Barbados, organized an African Masonic lodge to help his fellows. He also wanted to improve their minds by "searches and researches into men and things."[8] Shortly thereafter, in 1787, Richard Allen and Absalom Jones organized the Free African Society in Philadelphia as a protest to discrimination in the organized churches. The preamble to the Articles of Association states, in part, that these "two men of the African race, who for their religious life and conversion have obtained a good report among men . . . have from a love of the people of their own complexion whom they beheld in sorrow, because of their irreligious and uncivilized state,"[9] decided to form an organization to help themselves and to provide for their people's widows and fatherless children. This organization led inexorably to the founding of the African (Protestant Episcopal and Methodist Episcopal) churches which ascribed to the biblical maxim that "Princes shall come out of Egypt and Ethiopia shall soon stretch forth her hands unto God." This institution would later provide not only religious but also secular links between Africans in the diaspora and those on the continent. It would also stimulate both religious and political opposition to European rule in Africa.[10]

In 1787, stirred by the same sentiments that led the Reverends Allen and Jones to found the AME churches, a number of blacks organized the New York African Free School. This move stimulated the founding of a number of African schools throughout the North and a few in the South. These schools would later produce such graduates as Alexander Crummell and Henry Highland Garnet, men who fought for freedom for blacks in America and did everything in their power to establish links with Africa. Significantly, Paul Cuffee also founded one of these African schools in 1797 to improve the lot of blacks in America.[11] Toward the end, he turned his attention to emigration to Africa as a means of dealing with the plight of freedmen. Cuffee was to discover that blacks could not even go to Africa without the consent of the increasingly dominant Europeans. He, therefore, established contact with the African Institution in Britain. Starting in 1787, this philanthropic group had sponsored the emigration to Sierra Leone of the unwanted English black poor; the Afro-American supporters of Britain who had been stranded in Nova Scotia; some of the rebellious Jamaican Maroons who had been shipped to Nova Scotia; and the settling in Sierra Leone of a growing number of liberated slaves recaptured from ships taking them to the New World.

Cuffee visited Sierra Leone in 1811 to prepare the groundwork for taking American blacks to that country. While there he founded the Friendly Society of Sierra Leone "to open a channel of intercourse" between blacks in America and those in Sierra Leone. He also interested himself in education in this colony because he felt that "Africa calls for men of character to fill stations in the Legislature. . . ." But Cuffee found to his dismay that the War of 1812 frustrated his plan to take blacks to Sierra Leone. Finally, in 1815 and without the aid of either the European philanthropists or the American government, Cuffee transported thirty-eight persons to Freetown. The politics of race in the United States ended Cuffee's experiment, but he had taken the initiative of helping New World blacks to return to the African soil.[12]

Much to the chagrin and dismay of U.S. black leaders such as Paul Cuffee, Richard Allen, and Absalom Jones, white Americans created the American Colonization Society in 1816 to settle black Americans in what became known as Liberia. The whites were fulfilling a dream of many U.S. presidents, including Washington, Jefferson, Madison, and Monroe, who felt that blacks should be settled outside the boundaries of the country because they could never become full-fledged citizens of it. Black leaders resented this notion and became concerned that the emigration to Africa of talented freed persons would deny leadership to many millions of their brethren still enslaved.[13] These ideas led black leaders to take a highly jaundiced view of emigration and caused them to turn against Africa, against Africans, and even against the settlers. So strong was the reaction against emigration and the fear that after centuries of contributing to building America, free blacks would be shipped penniless across the sea, that black leaders sought to eliminate both symbolic and remembered ties to Africa. In desperation, they even suggested that those early institutions, designed to aid the emancipation of their fellows, change names. The very word *Africa* was to be chiseled from the marble above church doors. Blacks were urged to refer to themselves as *Negro*, *Colored*, and even *Brown Anglo-Saxons*—anything but *African*. All of the black leaders of the period such as Alexander Crummell, Martin Delany, Frederick Douglass, James Forten, Henry Highland Garnet, and the Grimké brothers took positions for or against emigration.[14]

Despite their conviction that whites did not have either the interest of Afro-Americans or Africa in mind when advocating emigration to Liberia, a number of blacks saw emigration as the solution to their problem and to that of Africa. Lott Carey gave up a successful ministry in Richmond, Virginia, to go to Liberia. He was convinced that he and his kind could exert a civilizing influence in Africa. He declared: "I am an African; and in this country, however meritorious my conduct and respectable my character, I cannot receive the credit due to either. I wish to go to a country where I shall be estimated by my merits, not by my complexion, and I feel bound to labour for my suffering race."[15]

Expressing similar views about his Africanness was John B. Russwurm, who was born in Jamaica, but like millions of West Indians before and after, felt that he could be of greater service to himself and to his race by emigrating to the United States rather than languishing in the Caribbean. Russwurm, one of the earliest black graduates of a white American university, entered the struggle for the abolition of slavery and founded *Freedom's Journal*, the first black newspaper. But like Lott Carey before him, Russwurm soon felt that it was in Africa rather than in the United States that the battle to free blacks should best be fought. Once in Liberia, he founded the *Liberia Herald* and held many important positions, including that of governor of the colony of Maryland.[16]

Although criticized for going to Africa and becoming a white-oriented elite, the Lott Careys, the Russwurms, and others in Liberia joined the so-called *Creoles* of Sierra Leone in educating the local people and in struggling for the equality of African peoples. They continued to provide links with New World blacks. Among the latter were Martin Delany and Robert Campbell, who as members of the African Civilization Society, undertook the Niger River Exploration Expedition. They had plans to obtain land from the Egba in Nigeria to plant a colony and to grow cotton for export.[17] Delany and Campbell established contact with leaders and black missionaries such as Samuel Ajayi Crowther among the Egbas, and with Russwurm, Alexander Crummell, and Edward W. Blyden in Monrovia. Delany returned to America, but Campbell returned to Lagos to edit a paper.

By the mid-nineteenth century there was an important network of New World blacks serving in West Africa. These included such persons as Joseph Smith, Henry Barnes, Charles Bannerman, and West Indian Thomas Hughes, who advised King Aggrey of the Fanti, then in conflict with the encroaching British. When the Fantis launched their federation to resist being taken over by the British, it was persons such as R. J. Ghartey, James F. Missah, James Hutton Brew, F. C. Grant, and Joseph Africanus Horton, a Sierra Leone staff surgeon then serving in the British Army in the Gold Coast, who drew up the constitution of this political entity. Similar groups of persons functioned in parts of Nigeria at this period.[18]

This network of men functioned not only in Africa, they sought active links with their counterparts in North America. For example, in 1863 President J. D. Johnson of Liberia sent Edward W. Blyden, born in St. Croix, Virgin Islands, and Alexander Crummell, an Afro-American, to act as commissioners to black Americans, inviting their "aid in building up a Negro nationality of freedom and Christianity on the continent of their ancestors." The especially prescient Blyden warned black leaders:

> Supposing that it were possible for black men to rise to the greatest eminence, in this country, in wealth and political distinction, so long as there is no Negro power of respectability in Africa, and that continent remained in her present degradation—she would reflect unfavorably upon them. . . . If no Negro state of respectability be erected in Africa—no Negro government permanently established in that land—then the prejudice in question will make its obstinate stand against all the wealth, and genius, and skill that may be exhibited by Negroes in North or South America. The work is to be done in Africa.[19]

Alexander Crummell, for his part, sincerely felt that the free blacks in America had duties toward Africa. He wrote to a friend:

> There seems to me to be a natural call upon the children of Africa in foreign lands, to come and participate in the opening of treasures of the land of their fathers. Though these treasures are the manifest gift of God to the Negro race, yet that race reaps but the most partial measure of their good and advantage. It has always been thus in the past, and now as the resources of Africa are being more and more developed, the extent of *our* interest therein is becoming more and more diminutive. . . . It is the duty of black men to feel and labour for the salvation of the mighty millions of their kin all through this continent.[20]

The Liberians had hoped that with the end of the Civil War and the beginning of the Reconstruction Era, Afro-Americans would play an important role in the politics of an America which was rapidly gaining power in the global system. Thanks, in part, to their personal support of presidential candidates, a number of Afro-American leaders gained diplomatic posts in Haiti and Liberia. Some of the ministers to Liberia openly advocated what they believed the American government and the Americo-Liberians ought to do in order to protect Liberia.

James M. Turner, the first minister to Liberia, after repeatedly requesting aid for Liberia, bluntly told Washington: "I deem it unnecessary to say to the Department that there can be no radiating force so potent in the civilizing and Christianizing of Africa as a Christian commonwealth, a religious Negro nationality, under the auspicious control of democratic institutions of government." Yet, Turner despaired that the Americo-Liberians had not come to grips with the indigenous populations.[21]

John Henry Smyth, a later diplomat, was even rebuked by a secretary of state for reporting that he had taken it upon himself to warn the Liberian president against taking too harsh a policy toward the interior populations. Smyth apparently felt that he could say such things to the Liberian president because he was trying his best to alert the State Department to the consequences for Liberia if the indigenous populations defected to the Europeans. Smyth sought help from the secretary of state to protect Liberian territory. He wrote:

> Denude Liberia of a portion of her territory, and she so far is injured and falls in the estimation of native races. Should England take the disputed territory, and the native races be forced into a recognition of a foreign, alien power, they will never *feel* any respect for it. The change must affect injuriously Liberia, and injuriously the aboriginal Negroes' self respect. The civilized Negro in Africa under foreign domination, as the civilized Negro out of Africa under like control, suffers in his liberty,

because it has not the element of imperium. "Imperium et Libertas" must be of the motto and the practice of the Negro, if he is to have self-respect; if he is to merit the respect of others. I hope it may be found in consonance with the foreign policy of our Government to aid Liberia in a retention of her self-respect unimpaired, her control of her territory, her prestige which is the consequence of her control.[22]

When news of the forthcoming Berlin Conference trickled down to Liberia, Smyth felt that the time had come to put the pressure on the department by going outside of it. On June 18, 1883, he enclosed a letter to John B. Latrobe, president of the American Colonization Society, in which he said that the territory in West Africa extending from Cape Palmas to San Pedro, the southernmost limit of Liberia, was unoccupied by any "civilized Liberians either as residents or transitory traders." Smyth feared that if the Liberians were not encouraged to move into this locality, there was the possibility that the local people might be induced to deny the authority of Liberia, and that the British government might be induced by the governor of the Gold Coast, or the governor in chief of the West African settlement, to "take the territory from Liberia in the interest of peace, civilization or trade." Smyth concluded:

> Should the society appreciate the importance of having the *Coast Line* of Liberia secure by civilized occupancy, as it is desirous of having the interior occupied and controlled by like influence, I would respectfully suggest that the attention of the Liberian government be at once directed to this matter which may produce a happy change in the present status of affairs which I conceive to be uncertain.[23]

The European imperial drive to carve up Africa that had been sanctioned by the Berlin Conference placed all African societies in jeopardy—even Liberia. Having agonized over the negotiations during which the United States mediated between an almost helpless Liberia and the aggressive British Lion, Minister Smyth sought to use the issue of Afro-American interest in Africa as a tool in dealing with the secretary of state on African affairs. He expressed the hope that with the reconstruction in the South, "it is not reasonable to anticipate any considerable exodus of that portion of the nation toward this or any other part of the orient." Nevertheless, he felt that the enlightened self-respect of some blacks would induce them to turn their attention to Africa, the habitat of their race. He suggested that those persons would take an interest in the work of civilization there, which would manifest itself by some seeking the country as missionaries, educational and evangelical, by others traveling there for commercial reasons, and by still others aiding the work of civilizing Africa through mission efforts at home.

Smyth then asked, rhetorically:

> May not these connections existent between Africans in Africa, and American-Africans represented in our country by millions, give the United States a hold upon the African continent, as a race link; should Liberia continue as a Negro state, more potent and permanent than Europe can ever have though its African interests be guarded by fleets and standing armies?

The minister concluded his cable to the secretary of state with the following words:

> The foregoing is suggested with direct reference to our interests as a great and growing nation, and with due regard to Liberia's interests. . . . I have to express the hope that our Government may find it within the scope of its foreign policy, and its friendly relations with the Republic to assist Liberia's successful passage through this crisis, which is probably the only one of serious moment that is likely to confront, and which threatens Liberia in the near or remote future.[24]

Seen in retrospect, there was little that a small but influential network of educated Africans, or even the African traditional leaders, could have done to forestall the partitioning of Africa. In fact, so powerful and determined to carve up Africa were the Europeans, that the people at Berlin not only ignored the concerns of Liberia, but required it to obey the rules governing the appropriation of African lands to which she was not a signatory power. Realizing that the attempt to "legitimate" commerce had failed and that the European companies (such as John Holt and the United Africa Company) and the French companies were quarreling not only with each other but with such African traders as Jaja or Opobo, the decision was made to integrate the African economies "into the expanding cash-based economies of Europe."

As ill luck would have it, the "scramble for Africa" coincided with the end of Reconstruction and what has been called the nadir of black Americans.[25] Not only could they not help themselves, they increasingly looked to Africa for their salvation. And as is often typical of people who have no political power to defend themselves, blacks increasingly activated missionary networks and used their religious institutions to help themselves and Africa. For example, Samuel Ajayi Crowther, who as a missionary was part of the influential Sierra Leonian Creole diaspora in West Africa and who went as a catechist with the British Niger Expedition in 1841–1842, stated that he was determined "to render some help, in the service of the Church Missionary Society, to my fellow creatures." He had hoped "that the time may come when the Heathen shall be fully given to Christ for His inheritance, and the uttermost part of the earth for His possession."[26] Meanwhile, in Liberia, Alexander Crummell, following in the footsteps of such earlier missionaries as Lott Carey, not only preached but used the church as a mechanism for the political salvation of Africa.

The activities of the Reverend William H. Sheppard in the Congo did much to vindicate the efforts of another Afro-American, the historian George Washington Williams, to publicize Leopold II's maladministration of that ravaged land. Visiting the Congo in 1890, Williams was scandalized by what he encountered. He leveled twelve specific charges against the king of the Belgians, concluding:

> Against the deceit, fraud, robberies, arson, murder, slave-raiding, and general policy of cruelty of your Majesty's Government to the natives, stands their record of unexampled patience, long-suffering and forgiving giving spirit, which put the boasted civilization and professed religion of your Majesty's Government to the blush. . . .
>
> All the crimes perpetrated in the Congo have been done in *your* name, and *you* must answer at the bar of Public sentiment for the misgovernment of a people, whose lives and fortunes were entrusted to you by the August Conference of Berlin, 1884–1885.[27]

Williams appealed to the International Commission to investigate the charges and to the Anti-Slavery Societies in all parts of Christendom to end the tragedy in the Congo. He asked the Constitutional Government of the Belgian people, "so proud of its traditions, replete with the song and story of its champions of human liberty, and so jealous of its present position in the Sisterhood of European States—to cleanse itself from the imputation of the crimes with which your Majesty's unlimited personal State of Congo is polluted." Finally, Williams, fearing that he would be misunderstood, called upon the "Heavenly Father, whose service is perfect love, in witness of the purity of my motives and the integrity of my aims; and to history and mankind I appeal for the demonstration and vindication of the truthfulness of the charge I have herein briefly outlined."[28] Apparently, in 1890 Williams also sent a "report upon the Congo-state and country to [the] President of the United States of America," but there is no evidence that the president had done anything about it before Williams died in 1891, one year later.

In 1890, the same year that Williams's reports were made public, Reverend Sheppard, a missionary, received a royal welcome from the Bakuba, who believed that his quick grasp of their language indicated "that his body must contain the spirit of some member of the tribe who was trying to return to them after death.[29] In 1897, Sheppard reported that the Zappo-Zap (Basonge) soldiers, used by the Europeans for tax-collection, were slave-raiding on behalf of the state and, in the process, were committing all sorts of atrocities. At the request of the missionaries an inquiry was made, but the responsible European officials were not punished.

Due, in large part, to Sheppard's report on the terrible events in the Congo, Morrison and Morel, a white missionary and white shipping clerk respectively, took up the issue. When Morrison returned to the United States in 1903, he aroused "the American Mission boards and their supporters to a sense of their responsibility towards the Congo peoples." [30] He persuaded the important General Assembly of the Presbyterian Church to send delegations to complain to both Secretary of State Hay and President Roosevelt. The missionaries also succeeded in getting J. T. Morgan of Alabama, a member of the Senate Committee on Foreign Relations and "a strong character, who often led rather than followed public opinion, to lend his considerable weight to the cause of Congo reform." [31] The memorial he presented to Congress appealed to the American government to intervene actively in Congo affairs. Morel, too, visited the United States to speak on the Congo question at the Boston Peace Conference of October 1904. Booker T. Washington, who had emerged as the most important black leader at that time and who had been a classmate of Sheppard when the two were students at Hampton Institute in Virginia, joined Morel at the Boston Peace Conference. He made a plea on behalf of "his brethren in the so-called Congo Free State but what is really the Congo Slave State." [32]

Faced with such powerful elite factions, the United States government tried to temporize. President Theodore Roosevelt, who had created a scandal by inviting Booker T. Washington to the White House, expressed "sympathetic interest" in the missionaries' struggle, but it seemed that the United States had no intention of committing itself. Secretary of State Hay even told Baron Moncheur, the Belgian minister, that the United States was not a signatory to the Berlin Act and therefore might not have been entitled to interfere in the Congo affair. In order to pacify blacks, the missionaries, and others, the State Department named Clarence Slocum consul-general to the Congo State. Pressure did not stop, however, and in December 1906 Senator Lodge introduced a resolution to Congress assuring President Roosevelt of Senate approval for any measure he might judge necessary to ameliorate conditions in the Congo. From this point on, Leopold was no longer able to count on American support, and the U.S. government backed the Belgian government's decision to annex the Congo State. [33]

Sheppard himself was apparently not satisfied that the Belgian State's policy in the Congo was much better than that of Leopold. In January 1908, he published an article in the *Kasai Herald* criticizing the treatment accorded the Bakuba by the Kasai Company, and the company charged him with libel. The missionaries challenged the right of the Congo courts to try American citizens, but they lost this battle, and the trial took place in Leopoldville in 1909. The trial itself aroused great interest in the United States, and the American Congo Reform Association did its utmost to see that the trial received full publicity. During the trial Sheppard, probably out of missionary zeal but perhaps out of complete identification with the Bakuba, stated that he was "no longer of England or America, but of the Kasai." He was acquitted along with his collaborators Vandervelde and Morrison. The last we hear of his activities is this plea to blacks in America: "So we beg of you that you lift up your eyes and see the fast ripening harvest field, and hear our soul's pleading cry, 'Come over into Macedonia, and help us.'"[34] Years later, the followers of the Prophet Simon Kimbangu would recall the help the Congolese people received from the black missionaries.

While black missionaries were using their network and influence to ameliorate the condition of the black man in Africa, and by extension in America, the African Methodist Episcopal Church was especially active in creating networks and branches in West, South, and East Africa for religious as well as political action. In South Africa in the 1870s, blacks increasingly became dissatisfied with the white churches. Then, in 1884, Nehemia Tile, a Wesleyan minister, established a church for the Tembu people, but these churches were frustrated by the absence of a link to a church with a duly consecrated bishop descended from St. Peter. Help came through a fortuitous network that had been established by a member of the Zulu Jubilee Singers, who had been stranded in America after the end of the Cotton State Exposition at Atlanta in 1895, rescued by an AME minister, and sent to Wilberforce University to be educated. This student (later Mrs. Maxeke) wrote back to South Africa and reported being hosted by a remarkable black church with its own clergy, including bishops. The South African separatists, now including a growing "Ethiopian Church," sent one of its representatives, James M. Dwane, to America "to consolidate the union of the Ethiopian Church and the AME Church." While in America, Dwane assured his black audiences "that the Africans would never allow the white man to ride roughshod over their country. Africans were rapidly inbibing civilized habits and would soon be able to run great civilized governments. Then they would say to the European nations, 'Hands off!'"[35]

One of the presiding bishops of the AME Church with whom Dwane sought affiliation was Henry McNeal Turner, a staunch "nationalist" and an "emigrationist." According to his own testimony, Turner had been converted to the cause of Africa after hearing a sermon by Bishop

Alexander Crummell, then on a visit home from Liberia. By 1860 Turner had been preaching sermons with titles such as, "The Redemption of Africa and the Means to be Employed," in which he insisted that Africa could, and should be encouraged to advance with the help of black colonists from the United States. The bishop was also present at the Atlanta exposition in 1896, where the Zulu Jubilee Dancers had performed, and he had engaged in a debate with a white showman and accused him of denigrating Africans in a program devoted to a "Dahomean Village."[36] Thus, it was with great joy and expectation that Bishop Turner and the AME church welcomed the South Africans into their fold. Turner consummated the relationship during a triumphal five-week visit to South Africa. Importantly, he was received courteously by President Paul Kruger of the Transvaal Republic and allegedly encouraged to evangelize blacks in the country. Later, reflecting upon this meeting, Turner concluded that "the President received our church with great cordiality, though I must confess, if reports be true, it was not so much from love of it as from distrust of white missionaries, whom he greatly disliked."[37]

What Kruger obviously did not know, or discounted, was that the AME church was structurally opposed to white domination of any sort. In time, both the Afrikaners (Boers) and the British would accuse the church of helping subversion in South Africa. During this period, many Afro-Americans identified with the plight of blacks in South Africa. For example, Bishop Coppin, who went to South Africa around the turn of the century, wrote copious letters about the situation there and requested help from black Americans. He implored them to:

> Pity them, pity them, Christians at home. We could begin the work at once, and what a blessing it would be. It is not at all likely that any more will be done for this class of natives by the Europeans than is being done. There is already a measure on foot—and it finds many advocates—to remove them to a location, that is to say, to get a camp outside of the city and place them there, where they will be beyond the reach of civilizing influences. The inevitable result, therefore, will be that under this plan they will remain perpetually in their present condition, though living under the very shadow of a civilized and Christian community. Once they owned all the land by inheritance, and now they are not permitted to domicile on it, or, only upon such portions of it as may be allotted to them out of pity.[38]

And he felt that

> when we are told that a man in America is denied civil and political rights on account of being a descendant of Africa, we are content to call it unjust, ungodly; but when we are told that an African in Africa is denied civil privileges because he is an African, we feel that besides

being unrighteous and unworthy of our Christian civilization, it is ridiculous in the extreme.

Like many blacks of the period, Bishop Coppin also felt that

there is but one right thing for the African, Africander, Afro-world wider or colored man by whatever distinguishing title, to do; and that is to unite in an effort to prove that merit does not inhere in color, but with common attributes, the whole human family, under proper conditions, is capable of reflecting the image of God and rising to that dignity of which mankind alone is capable.

When the Anglo-Boer War broke out in 1898, blacks in the AME church and elsewhere agonized about the plight of the Africans and used their network to render assistance. Frederick J. Loudin, director of the eminent Fisk Jubilee Singers, wrote from London to John Edward Bruce ("Bruce Grit"), a journalist and activist in African and Afro-American affairs, that

the white people are holding meetings all over the country passing resolutions of sympathy with those Boers who would enslave our people the very moment they free themselves from British rule. In fact it is well known that it is Britain's refusal to allow this that is in a great measure responsible for the present outbreak. I grant you that British rule in South Africa is not all we wish it were, but it is a thousand times better than Boer administration. Britain has her missionaries there and doing something to lift up the race while the Boers with all their religious hypocrisy don't believe we even have a soul to be saved and only seek to repress and further degrade us.[39]

Loudin implored blacks to take an overt stand on the war:

That which I would advise and *strongly* too is that mass meetings be held, resolutions—of which our people are very fond of passing—be passed and sent to the British Ambassador or to Lord Salisbury, but if sent to the British Ambassador requesting him to forward them to his government and don't be afraid to make them too strong and let them know *who* we are.

Please do not delay for *now* is the time. We will, I am sure in this way make more friends—and God knows we need them—than in any other way. It will influence the treatment of our race in Africa as well; the opportunity is one of a lifetime. It is the one time when the expression of opinion will have great weight.[40]

The British won the war, but the Boers won the peace, and as all blacks had feared, the plight of the Africans worsened. The AME church missionaries returned to South Africa after the war and were implicated when in 1906, the Africans in Natal, led by Chiefs Gobizemberk, Dinizulu, and Bambata rebelled against discrimination. The whites blamed the Ethiopian movement, the AME church, and Africans educated in America for the uprising. The *Natal Mercury,* a newspaper, declared: "An evil star rose in the American firmament and sent its satellites to preach sedition in Natal." One witness testified "that Natal Natives were being sent to colleges in America. Over 150 young Natives were recently sent from South Africa, including twenty from Natal. This was one of the greatest dangers to the standing of the white men in South Africa." The witness added that "he would be loath to hinder any man getting education, but the fact to which he had drawn attention was a great danger to their future."[41] Of course, the evil lay not in the "stars" of the "American firmament" but in the bosom of South African society itself. What blacks in America did was to provide the support for those Africans who were willing to struggle for their freedom. Many of those Africans who had come into contact with the black churchmen and missionaries formed the nucleus of the South African Native National Congress. Black American missionaries also had an input into the John Chilembwe Rising that occurred years later in Nyasaland.[42]

What is quite clear, then, is that blacks, especially those in the United States of America, sought to take advantage of the opportunities opened to them to attempt to ameliorate their own position and that of their fellows on the African continent. They had the unique, if often the dubious, distinction of being in what has often been called, "the belly of the beast," in an America that was destined to inherit the mantle of European dominance. From this vantage point they were often able to inaugurate the networks and create the institutions that served their cause and that of Africans at a period when most continental Africans were unable to do so, or did not need to do so. What is significant about early black diplomats in Liberia is that their efforts, while important to the future of that "black nationality," remained largely unknown and unsung. The result has been that later generations of blacks, both on the continent and in the diaspora, have been led to believe that there was less cooperation between their ancestors than was indeed the case. The two later periods of black networking, the Pan-African phase and the contemporary phase are better known, but there is the need to put all of the phases of black cooperation in global perspective.

NOTES

1. Elliott P. Skinner, "Afro-Americans and the African Dispersal," in a symposium on *The African Dispersal: Expectations and Realities,* sponsored by the Afro-American Studies Center, Boston University, 1979, 5-33; C. L. R. James, *A History of Pan-African Revolt,* (Washington, D.C.: Drum and Spear Press, 1969); Sylvia M. Jacobs, *The African Nexus: Black American Perspectives on the European Partitioning of Africa, 1880–1920* (Westport, Conn.: Greenwood Press, 1981).
2. Philip D. Curtin, *Africa Remembered: Narratives by West Africans from the Era of the Slave Trade,* (Madison: University of Wisconsin Press, 1968).
3. Eric Williams, *Capitalism and Slavery,* (Chapel Hill: University of North Carolina Press, 1944).
4. Marion D. B. Kilson, "Towards Freedom: An Analysis of Slave Revolts in the United States," *Phylon* 25 (2nd Quarter, 1964): 175–187; Herbert Aptheker, *American Negro Slave Revolts* (New York: International Publishers, 1963).
5. David Brion Davis, *The Problem of Slavery in the Age of Revolution, 1770–1823* (Ithaca: Cornell University Press, 1975), 173, 273.
6. Leslie H. Fisher, Jr., and Benjamin Quarles, *The Negro American: A Documentary History* (Glenview, Ill.: Scott, Foresman and Co., 1967), 76ff, 7.
7. John Hope Franklin, *From Slavery to Freedom* (New York: Vintage Books, 1969), *passim.*
8. Fisher and Quarles, *op. cit.,* 76–77.
9. *Loc. cit.*
10. George Shepperson, "Notes on Negro American Influences on the Emergence of African Nationalism," *Journal of African History,* vol. 1, no. 2, (1960): 304ff.
11. Herbert Aptheker, ed., *A Documentary History of the Negro People in the United States,* vol. 1 (New York: Citadel Press, 1951), 109.
12. Theodore Draper, *The Rediscovery of Black Nationalism* (New York: Viking Press, 1979), 16–18 and *passim.*
13. Philip J. Staudenraus, *The African Colonization Movement, 1816–1865* (New York: Columbia University Press, 1961).
14. *Loc. cit.*
15. Carter G. Woodson, *Negro Orators and Their Orations* (Washington, D.C.: Associated Publishers, 1925), 80ff.
16. Draper, *op. cit.,* 10.
17. Victor Ullman, *Martin R. Delaney: The Beginnings of Black Nationalism* (Boston: Beacon Press, 1971), 152ff.
18. *Ibid.,* 273–274.
19. Hollis Lynch, ed., *Selected Letters of Edward W. Blyden* (New York: K. T. O. Press, 1971), 290–291; Adelaide Cromwell Hill and Martin Kilson, eds., *Apropos of Africa: Sentiments of American Negro Leaders on Africa From the 1800s to the 1950s* (London: Frank Cass and Co., 1969), 48.
20. August Meier, ed., *Negro Thought in America: 1880–1915* (Ann Arbor: University of Michigan Press, 1963), 33.
21. *Dispatches from United States Ministers to Liberia,* 15 January 1872, Micro-Copy No. 170, National Archives, Washington, D.C.
22. Minister John H. Smyth to Secretary of State Steward, 7 August 1897, *Dispatches from United States Ministers to Liberia, 1852–1906,* No. 326, Record Group 59, Roll 3, National Archives, Washington, D.C.
23. Hill and Kilson, *op. cit.,* 94–97.
24. *Loc. cit.*

25. Rayford W. Logan, *The Negro in American Life and Thought: The Nadir, 1877–1901* (New York: Dial Press, 1954).
26. *African Repository* (October 1968): 313.
27. Ruth M. Slade, "English-Speaking Missions in the Congo Independent State: 1878– 1908," *Academie royale des Sciences coloniales, Classe des Sciences Morales, et Politiques,* Memoires in 80. N.S. Tome 16, fasc. 2 et denier, Bruxelles (1959): 105ff.
28. *Loc. cit.;* Jacobs, *op. cit.,* 80ff.
29. "The Congo Atrocities," *The Southern Workman,* vol. 33, no. 5 (May 1904): 261–262.
30. Slade, *op. cit.,* 254.
31. *Ibid.,* 307–308.
32. Louis R. Harland and Raymond W. Smock, eds., *The Booker T. Washington Papers,* vol. 8, 1904–1906 (Urbana: University of Illinois Press, 1979): 85–94, 110, 203, 378, 482–484.
33. Slade, *op. cit.,* 309–313, 359, 371–372.
34. William H. Sheppard, "Yesterday, To-day, and To-morrow in Africa," *The Southern Workman,* vol. 39, no. 8 (August 1910): 477; Slade, *op. cit.*
35. J. Mutero Chirenje, "The Afro-American Factor in Southern African Ethiopianism, 1890–1986." Unpublished ms., 6.
36. Edwin S. Redkey, *Black Exodus* (New Haven: Yale University Press, 1969), 182; Anthony Ngube, "Contribution of the Black American Church to the Development of African Independent Movements in South Africa," in *For Better or Worse: The American Influence in the World,* ed. Allen F. Davis (Westport, Conn.: Greenwood Press, 1981), 146.
37. Edwin S. Redkey, ed., *Respect Black: The Writings and Speeches of Henry McNeal Turner* (New York: Arno Press and the New York Times, 1971), 179.
38. Hill and Kilson, *op. cit.,* 247ff.
39. *Ibid.,* 122–125
40. *Loc. cit.*
41. Edward Roux, *Time Longer Than Rope* (Madison: University of Wisconsin Press, 1966), 98.
42. George Shepperson and Thomas Price, *Independent African* (Edinburgh: Edinburgh University Press, 1958), 87ff; Roux, *op. cit., passim;* Karen E. Fields, *Revival and Rebellion in Colonial Central Africa* (Princeton: Princeton University Press, 1985), *passim.*

Response

E. U. Essien-Udom

IT is befitting that this first seminar, the first dialogue of the type initiated by the three universities—the University of Liberia, the University of Sierra Leone, and Boston University—is being held here in Liberia. I was struck this morning when Madam Chairman said that often we have tended to ignore the significance of the establishment of the Republic of Liberia and the revolution in Haiti in the struggle for achieving the status of modern nation-states among the blacks of the world, both on the continent and outside of this continent. I think this is quite true, and a great many—through certain disparaging allegations and through the ghosts of old, former political powers who controlled and continue to control from their borders the means of communication in our world today—are responsible. Consequently, Liberia has not gained the significance that she ought to have enjoyed in this struggle. Liberia is still looked upon with pity and sometimes with ridicule.

I shall now move on and try to comment on this excellent exposition by Dr. Skinner on the networks that have existed historically. I think a great many of us, in a curious way, through our reading, sometimes through our general knowledge, and sometimes through our understanding about these networks, appreciate quite fully that there has never been any real period, any real time, when either the elites or groups tending to be the intellectuals (be they in the church, in the universities, in the New World and the Old World) have not been in constant communication to find ways of obliterating the conditions that have affected the African people in the continent and outside the continent since the last century. I want to make one remark before I say anything more. Although these dialogues have always been carried on at the elite level, we should also mention another form of dialogue:

32

a representative-type dialogue, a network expressing the interests of the masses, the downtrodden, not of the elite per se. When we talk about the various Pan-African congresses, we tend to ignore this other form of dialogue, which represents Pan-Africanism at the grassroot level and which began—more intercontinentally—activities even as late as the second decade of this century and which were at work until the death of Garvey in 1940. The historians, I think, should correct this perspective that only the Pan-African congresses worthy of recognition were those of the elite. I think that is a distortion. Nkrumah, after the independence of Ghana in 1957, appreciated the need to recognize other meetings. The first Conference of Independent African States, convened in Ghana in 1958, represented the new elite, who had emerged in the postindependence period, were now in control of political power and the new states, and who were the defenders of the people. However, Nkrumah convened another conference, the All-African Peoples' Congress, which included the non-elite—church leaders, writers, and so forth.

I continue my remarks with the preposition that our subordination, our dependence in the past and in the present is economic. I do not think we would have reached this perspective from Dr. Skinner's paper, nor from most of the presentations at conferences like this, because, if you look at the slave trade as Eric Williams has done (or as Samir Amin would prefer) slavery was literally just another form of labor—politically and economically determined. We did not go, we were not exported to America to learn new civilization, to learn new culture, to learn how to sport, how to run and dance. We were not exported out there to be Christianized. We were exported out there for one purpose only. We were exported there to help, under forced conditions, completely forced, to develop new lands in the interest of the states of Europe. It was the new mercantilist period, when state power was being established. And if we have had problems in Africa, most of these problems have had to do with attempts to establish state power.

I think we have other problems when the military comes in and attempts to establish state power before developing anything else. Whether they do it well or partly, we need not say. But, you will notice, one of the things the military attempts to establish is state power. In the mercantilist period, we were the instruments. The Africans who were exported during this epoch to North America, Latin and South America, and to the Caribbean were the instruments of establishing state power in the mercantilist period of Europe, and they were no more than economic instruments. In Africa, it is true that during this period we continued to enjoy a measure of apparent autonomy up until the formal partitioning of most of Africa. But soon, through that triangular trade, our labor was expropriated to accumulate capital in Europe—through the mines, the minerals, the tobacco, the sugar, and the cotton that would later feed Lancaster mills. Europeans were building their state power at our expense, and what did we get in return? Gin. We got some flashly cloth in return. We got handcuffs for capturing him or her by both legs and arms, dumping those we captured into one of those boats lying about. We saw them sent, finally, to the ships, and we heard of the passage and of the wharves of South America and the Islands.

This period was a great period of state development, the development of state power in Europe and America. But in Africa, I think even by 1800, beginning with that trade, we had been drawn into Europe in a different and most significant way over a period of time before formal colonialism. We were drawn into the system of consuming the products and the goods of Europe, the system of being the consumers of the goods of Europe, particularly the material goods. The availability of cheap cotton material replaced the need for skill associated with cloth-making, in West Africa and elsewhere. The Europeans brought goods, and they worked cleverly: first they gave us goods, and as we began to consume these goods, formal colonialism was established with capitalism. Now what seemed strong, gaining in favor, expanding more rapidly, knowing neither God nor man, was profit—the rule of gold. Under the informal reign of this new economy, Europe established empires—Portugal, Britain, France, and so forth. Today, they have established state power through the scientific breakthroughs, the technology, and superior organization. They were able to gain a militant stature by wielding political domination and economic power through economic exploitation. So the two of us—whether you were left at home or whether you were exported—were the instruments not only of the building up of state power in Europe, but also of the building up of the economic power and the higher and higher standards of living in Europe.

In this network we have not said very much about the efforts made to deal with this problem. The Garvey movement added a very important dimension—how we could achieve self-reliance by turning around the old triangular trade and getting the three groups of us—in North and South America, Africa, and the Caribbean—to come into an economic relationship which could ameliorate our dependence. So far, we have not succeeded in finding a way of dealing with this problem, a problem which is derived from the whole issue of being deprived of a great deal of both initiative and of autonomy in development. Today, we are all involved in consuming the latest and highest development technology of Europe, particularly our elites in the old parts of the world. The consuming elements have made us dependent; the political factor was like having infantry on the ground. So we have not appraised sufficiently those years and the networks, except those of Garvey, Duse Mohammed, and a few other people we recall. We have not appraised the course of our dependence, of our subordination. The one single cartel that blacks of the world possessed, the one economic power, was slavery—and that is it. We are dependents, subordinates, within the capitalistic framework, first as slaves, later as consumers of Europe's goods.

So I shall end these very brief remarks as I started, by saying that our subordination was economic, our dependency is economic, especially on the continent of Africa. It has different consequences for the diaspora within the nation-states like the United States. They, too, experience it; when unemployment comes and the average for the nation is 10 percent, the average for blacks is likely to be 25 percent. When the national average might be 10 percent or 12 percent, it is always greater for blacks.

In Africa, because of the way we think we are modernizing—that's a nonsense term, really nonsense terms, *developing* and *modernizing*. In what way? Who is developing? The barbarians run around the world, kill and abandon, whether in Vietnam or in Afghanistan or where have you. Having the means of killing women—is that development? I do not think those terms are adequate, really. When we think of what development is and what it is not, we shall find the level of development is civilization, whether it is Western European or American civilization. Another element of development is the African context and among the African peoples. In the period of our independence, in Africa and in the Caribbean, what do we see in the name of development, in the name of modernization? Our economic dependency has become greater because we are so linked with the system of consumption as against production. That brings to us those attributes of Europe, including the decadent aspects of contemporary European civilization, which even in their societies represent deviant behavior. I am thinking of the widespread consumption of something called morphine in the African continent today by the elite—the upper elite classes who can afford to buy this kind of thing. So, while we think we are developing, we are becoming more dependent economically, and our economic crisis will deepen and will continue to deepen as our pattern of development continues to follow the lines which were laid in the period of mercantilism in Europe, the period of development of state power in Europe.

The World Economy and the African/ Afro-American Connection

Ali A. Mazrui

THE black American is a product of the world economy, at least in the first instance. This particular human category would not be where it is were it not for the twists and turns of global market forces over a period of at least three centuries. During that period, those market forces have been capitalist-dominated.

If the black American is thus a product of the world economy and of the evolution of world capitalism, we cannot fully understand the African/Afro-American Connection without attempting to understand the interplay between the world economy and the black peoples in a historical perspective. Those who were later to become black Americans started their trans-Atlantic destiny as specimens of African labor. One question that now arises is whether, by the last quarter of the twentieth century, they are beginning to become symbols of American capital. Are the descendants of African slaves of yesteryears now becoming the American investors of tomorrow?

Before we can grapple satisfactorily with such questions, it is indeed important to put the African/Afro-American Connection in the context of global economic history. There was a period when the most important resource that Africa had, from the point of view of Western needs, was labor. This was the period that produced the slave trade, which in turn resulted in the emergence of the black American as a new entity on the world scene. This can be called the period of the *labor imperative* in the relationship between the world economy and the African peoples.

Then, there came a time when Africa's most important resource for the West was deemed to be territory. This produced the new imperialism, which strangely enough, was allied to abolitionism and new forms of Western humanitarianism. This can be called the period of the *territorial imperative* in the relations between the world economy and the African peoples.

As colonization matured and consolidated, a new and related imperative was emerging: *industrial minerals and energy resources.* These had become Africa's most important resources from a Western perspective.

The fourth phase in the interaction between world economic forces and people of Africa and of African ancestry is the emerging imperative of *black purchasing power and black investment.* In this phase, what the West sells to Africa or to people of African ancestry is becoming at least as important as what the West buys, plunders, or steals from black lands. Also in this phase, the idea of Africa as a place for foreign or white investment is being supplemented by the growing idea of Africans and people of African ancestry as active investors in their own right and not simply effected objects of investment by other people. Let us take each of these phases in turn as we explore the ramifications and implications of Africa's interaction with the world economy across time.

Black Destiny and World Labor

To some extent, race-consciousness in Europe was a parallel development to the evolution of both the nation-state and capitalism. The Protestant Reformation resulted, in part, in the emergence of national churches and the decline of the centralizing power of the Vatican in European affairs. Europe plunged into new forms of sectionalism and factionalism, which seemed, in part, to be reinforcing national and regional loyalties. Then came the Thirty Years War and the Treaty of Westphalia of 1648, which helped to lay the foundations of the state system and the principles of national sovereignty. This secularization of allegiance (to the state rather than to the church) led to the secularization of identity—nations and races became more visible as categories than religious orders. At the same time, capitalism was emerging, fed, and sustained to some extent by the new "Protestant ethic," with its emphasis on enterprise, on acquisitiveness without excessive consumption, on industriousness and individual accountability, and on the ethic of saving and investment rather than the older Christian ethic of charity.

Later on, whole new theories of racial gradation and ethnic stratification came into being, partly sustained by both capitalism and the new forms of European nationalism. In time, black peoples were relegated to the lowest levels of human stratification. The stage was set for the African slave trade, the midwife to the birth of the black American as a new human entity.

The seventeenth century marked a particular escalation of the trans-Atlantic slave trade. There is a raging debate about the figures of the trade and its general scale and extent.[1] One estimate argues that until the year 1600, considerably fewer than half a million slaves from West Africa had landed in the Americas. But during the course of the seventeenth century alone, that number was multiplied more than five times over. The eighteenth century became particularly devastating, witnessing the landing of some 6,050,000 black slaves from West Africa. This number is quite apart from the millions who perished either in the original hunt for slaves or in the middle passage of the Americas.

But what had increased the demand for slaves from the seventeenth century to the end of the eighteenth? The most important factor was the growth of labor-intensive forms of agriculture in the Americas. The earlier phases of this development were particularly influenced by Europe's sweet tooth. A whole chapter in the relations between the world economy and black peoples' concerns involves, quite simply, the impact of sugar on those relations. The cultivation of sugar in the New World and its expanding popularity in Europe and among white peoples were important factors behind the initial escalation of the slave trade, just as the importance of spices, both for taste and for preserving food, was part of the initial European penetration into Asia.

In time, expanding economies of the Americas themselves provided additional causes of the expansion of the trans-Atlantic slave trade. This expansion in the Americans is quite apart from that which took place during the earlier phases of the Industrial Revolution in Europe, which witnessed the growth of textile industries and the need for cotton and other cash crops, partly cultivated in the New World.

Britain was a major participant in this trans-Atlantic commercial phenomenon. By the end of the eighteenth century, British ships were carrying nearly half the slaves taken to the Americas. Britain's share of the slave trade was partly a reflection of her ascendancy in maritime commercial activities among European states and partly a measure of her access to the markets of the New World, especially in the Caribbean and North America. It is also arguable that the British share in the slave trade was enhanced by the fact that the parts of West Africa that Britain was beginning to control (especially the coast between the Gold Coast and the Niger Delta) were relatively thickly populated and, economically, the best developed in the area, as contrasted with the French-controlled areas of the Senegal-Gambia and the Sudan, which were more sparsely populated.

But then a somewhat strange historical phenomenon began to occur. Britain, which had been the leading slave-trading nation in the world, began to emerge as the leading abolitionist power. In time, British ships were sailing the high seas to thwart slave dealers. A crusade against the slave trade, and ultimately against slavery itself, emerged from the British Isles onto the stage of world history. The leading dealer in slaves, the leading capitalist power of the age had now become the leading abolitionist power. What were the reasons for this seeming paradox in Britain's historical role?

First, it would seem that while the earlier phases of capitalism favored the institution of slavery and invoked the imperative of labor as a justification for raiding Africa for slaves, the more advance stages of capitalism recognized slavery as ultimately less efficient than wage labor. After all, wages needed to be paid only in proportion to a laborer's work and, to some extent, in proportion to his productivity. But the cost of maintaining a slave did not need to be in proportion to that slave's work. Thus, sacking a lazy wage laborer was an effective method of getting rid of unproductive workers, whereas letting a lazy slave die without food was an expensive way of dealing with one's own property.

Second, the institution of slavery necessitated a welfare system for slaves who were too old to work and for babies and children who were too young to be productive. Wage labor, on the other hand, need not carry that additional baggage of family handouts for the workers, at least not in the eighteenth and nineteenth centuries.

Third, the Industrial Revolution and the agrarian revolutions had both destabilized the countryside in the Western world itself, and sent large numbers of rural folk trekking to urban centers for work. The countryside was becoming depopulated in the wake of mechanization and enclosure movements on land newly acquired by the rich for rural farming, animal husbandry, or plantation agriculture. The availabilty of displaced European countryfolk for wage labor obviated the necessity of seeking labor from distant Africa.

Finally, alongside the maturation of capitalism was the emergence of new liberalism in Europe and the North American areas. This new liberalism, with its concern for individual work and closer public accountability on the part of institutions of power, made the populations of the West increasingly responsive to the humanitarian message. Liberalism is to some extent a child of capitalism in Western history, but liberalism, in turn, is a sister to the humanitarian impulse. The alliance of the sisters helped to create a more responsive atmosphere to the trumpet call of abolition. The fact that slavery was, in any case, no longer necessary for national prosperity gave an added boost to this humanitarian movement.

Two long-term monuments to this new humanitarianism are the Republic of Liberia and Sierra Leone. Both were, in part, products of the effort to resettle in Africa those whom the West had transplanted from Africa. The American Colonization Society, committed to the repatriation of free blacks to Africa, was particularly active from 1816 to 1847. The term *colonization* in this context was seen as voluntary, induced, or forced repatriation. Thomas Jefferson was one of the earliest proponents of sending blacks to Africa. Abraham Lincoln was also interested in the idea, convinced as he was that although blacks did not deserve to be slaves, they did not deserve to be Americans either. Lincoln sponsored two efforts during the American Civil War to promote emigration of freed slaves to the Caribbean and Central America.

Some of the reasons for this repatriation were indeed humanitarian, while others were plainly racist. There was a strong sentiment of racial separatism, a belief that races were meant to be culturally distinct and, as far as possible, exclusive of each other. But liberal Americans also believed in a tradition of asylum and sanctuary. After all, the persecuted in the Old World had fled to America for refuge. Should not the persecuted in America, especially blacks, flee back to their own Old World?

There was also a doctrine which was a kind of black Zionism. Just as the Jews had dreamt of returning to Palestine, should not black Americans conspire to return to Africa? After all, American blacks comprised the only segment of society living in the United States under duress, imported against their will. Were they entitled to a "law of return" comparable to that which later attempted to open the gates of Israel to Jews from all over the world?

Finally, there is just the factor of escapism behind the repatriation venture. In promoting the idea of establishing a Liberia abroad, were white Americans simply seeking to export their "Negro Problem"? Were the black Americans who agreed or felt induced to go to Liberia simply seeking to escape their frustrations and indignity within the United States?

Whatever the reason, Liberia was born of an attempt to reverse the flow of history. Africa had helped the first phases of the capitalist-dominated world economy by providing some of the crucial labor for production. Now that slave labor was longer needed, should not the African workers be sent home? Like E. T., the black American was in America unwillingly.[2] But unlike E. T., the black American could not effectively "phone home." The founding of the American Colonization

Society was an effort to transport the black American back home, a modest attempt to reverse the older forces of the labor imperative in relations between the world economy and the African peoples.

The Territorial Imperative and Africa's Partitioning

As the abolitionist movement pushed forward toward its climax in the Western world, a new threat to Africa began to emerge. The specter of imperialism cast its shadow on the black man's continent. Again, the same Britain that was leading the world in the struggle against the slave trade and slavery itself was soon to lead the world in stealing the lands of blacks. The greatest abolitionist power was becoming the greatest imperialist power.

Indeed, the struggle against the slave trade was sometimes used as the pretext for the imperial annexation of African territories. In West Africa, establishing British administration was designed, in part—at least ostensibly—as a "mop-up operation" to end slave raids and the institution of slavery itself. In East Africa, British colonization was rationalized, in part, by the struggle against the Arab slave trade in that part of the continent. To save a few thousand Africans from one kind of enslavement, millions of others had to be subjected to the chains of colonialism.

In fairness, however, the abolitionist movement, indeed achieved some important gains. The scale of the trans-Atlantic slave trade in the nineteenth century was down to one-third of what it had been in the eighteenth century. Had the abolitionist movement been delayed by another century and had the United States continued to be a major importer of slaves, today blacks might well comprise one quarter of the total U.S. population. This would indeed have increased black leverage on American institutions in subsequent decades after Emancipation, but there would have been, of course, a cost to Africa and to those specific blacks who had to endure the indignity of bondage prior to Emancipation.

With British capitalism now hostile to slavery but favorable to imperialism, African lands were being annexed. Before long, the Union Jack was flying from the Niger Delta in the West to the source of the Nile in East Africa, and from Cairo in the North to Cape Town in South Africa.

Other colonizers of Africa included France, especially in West and Equatorial Africa; Belgium, especially in the Congo (now Zaire); Portugal, in Angola, Mozambique, and Guinea-Bissau; Italy, in part of Somalia and Libya; Spain, in the western Sahara; people of Dutch descent in South Africa; and, for a while, Germany in Tanganyika,

Cameroon, Togo, and South West Africa (now called Namibia by most of the world). But in this partitioning of Africa, Britain got the biggest chunk. Today, Nigeria alone has more people than the whole of French-speaking West and Equatorial Africa added together.

The disproportionate role played by Great Britain in both Africa and North America contributed one important bond to the African/ Afro-American Connection—the bond of the English language. Trans-Atlantic Pan-Africanism has been, overwhelmingly, a political phenomenon of an English-speaking black world. The founding fathers from the Americas have been such English-speaking black nationalists as Marcus Garvey of Jamaica, George Padmore of Trinidad, and W. E. B. Du Bois of the United States. The greatest African Pan-Africanist of this century was probably the English-speaking Ghanaian, Kwame Nkrumah. The most important cases of black Zionism, of former slaves returning to Africa, are Liberia and the Creole population of Sierra Leone. Both Liberia and Sierra Leone are, of course, English-speaking African countries.

The Pan-African movement was initially led by diaspora blacks such as Padmore, Garvey, and Du Bois, but at a critical meeting in Manchester in 1945, Pan-Africanism started to be Africanized in the sense that it was being primarily led by Africans who were born in Africa. Two people at the Manchester Congress who were later to be founder-presidents of their respective countries were Kwame Nkrumah of Ghana and Jomo Kenyatta of Kenya. According to the records, there was only one French-speaking black at the meeting in Manchester, and he was relatively marginal to the deliberations. Manchester was itself an English-speaking city in an English-speaking imperial power, and the blacks who assembled were primarily English speakers.

Twenty-nine years later, a Pan-African congress was actually held within Africa—in Dar es Salaam, Tanzania. Dar es Salaam was, of course, an English-speaking capital city, as well as a Swahili-speaking one. And the deliberations of the congress in 1974 revealed, once again, Anglophone leadership.

Two questions arise about this aspect of the history of Pan-Africanism. Why was the movement led by diaspora blacks from the late nineteenth century to 1945? Second, why has the movement been dominated, disproportionately, by English speakers? Let us take each of these two questions in turn.

Diaspora leadership in the first half of the century was due, in part, to the fact that black Americans and blacks in Europe had greater freedom of organization on issues like Pan-Africanism than did Africans in the colonies on the continent. Marcus Garvey organized a movement in the United States which at one stage could claim a following of up to six million people. Nothing of that scale was feasible in a colonized territory for much of the first half of the twentieth century, though the colonial atmosphere did improve after World War II to some extent. A second reason for diaspora leadership in the first half of the twentieth century was that the international horizons of black American elites as compared with African elites in this period were wider. A third reason was the greater racial and cultural aliena- tion of diaspora blacks, which led to a more compelling need to empathize with ancestry and to bridge the gap between spiritual alienation and political commitment. A related reason was the deeper race consciousness of diaspora blacks as compared with Africans on the continent. There is little doubt that black Americans, especially, are more race conscious than the average African on the continent. The preoccupation with racial issues among black Americans was itself an aspect of the fertile ground for diaspora leadership in the Pan-African movement.

But why has it been primarily the English-speaking portions of the diaspora that have been so active in the movement? Part of the answer lies, once again, in the size and nature of the United States in the world system. The visibility of almost all major American movements helps to give those movements greater attention than they would have commanded had they emerged elsewhere. The fact that the United States is an English-speaking country becomes relevant for the influence of American movements on others abroad. One must also consider the interplay between American racism and American liberalism. American racism causes among its blacks greater alienation than perhaps Brazilian racism causes among blacks in Brazil. On the other hand, American liberalism permitted, even in those earlier years, greater freedom of political organization among its blacks than might occur in Brazil. What this means is that Brazil was at once less racist than the United States and less liberal. By being less racist it caused lower levels of alienation; but by being less liberal it, in any case, denied blacks as well as whites, the level of political organization that the United States, even in the first half of the twentieth century, often afforded its own oppressed citizens. Again, the fact that Amer- ican blacks were English-speaking was a contribution toward the Anglicization of the Pan-African movement.

A related reason was that Portuguese colonies in Africa had less freedom of speech and organization than British colonies. The possi- bility of bonds of political Pan-Africanism between Angolans and Mozambicans on the one hand and black Brazilians on the other was considerably more restricted than the possibility of political ties between Nigerians and Ghanaians on one side and black Americans on the other.

Then there are the peculiarities of the French influence. On the one hand, French-speaking diaspora blacks are only a very small minority of the total number of diaspora blacks. French colonies in black areas in the Americas were limited to islands in the Caribbean. On the other hand, within Africa, France was the second largest imperial power. This imbalance between France's holdings of small islands in the Caribbean and its large presence in Africa made trans-Atlantic linkages weak. Moreover, the status of these islands as departments of metropolitan France, which empowered them to send deputies of their own to French parliamentary institutions, provided an integrationist allegiance for many blacks in the Caribbean, enabling them to identify with France in a more immediate sense than they might identify with Africa. This is in spite of the eloquent voices of such Pan-Africanists as Aimé Césaire of Martinique and his compatriot Franz Fanon.

Then there is the texture of the cultural influence of France, not only in its departments in the Caribbean but also in the former French colonies in Africa. Even when the French colonial subjects were Pan-Africanists, the nature of their Pan-Africanism tended to be more cultural than political, more concerned with the vindication of African traditions than with the pursuit of African political independence. Francophone Africans have, therefore, tended to be much more alive and active in Pan-African cultural festivals as opposed to Pan-African political debates and political struggles. *Négritude* as a movement is basically Pan-Africanist but ultimately in the literary and artistic fields. The African prophet of *Négritude*, former President Léopold Senghor of Senegal, could at once affirm the virtues of African traditions and still be one of the greatest lovers of France. What all this means is that the French cultural impact tended to depoliticize Pan-Africanism among French-speaking Africans and to convert the nationalist emotions away from political organization and demands for independence toward an emphasis on cultural identity.

Yet another reason for political Pan-Africanism being dominated so disproportionately by English speakers is the importance of the English language within southern Africa, the last bastion of racism on the continent. Apart from Mozambique and Angola, almost the entire subregion of southern Africa, comprising more than ten states, is primarily English-speaking. South Africa is indeed dominated by Dutch-speaking whites, but the primary European language of the black majority is English rather than Afrikaans. The majority of the front-line states are English speakers, and the leader, Tanzania, under Julius Nyerere, is also English-speaking in this sense. Since the last great struggles for African liberation in Namibia and South Africa are going to be waged by liberation movements led by English-speaking Africans, the clarion call of nationalism in the continent will continue to be disproportionately Anglophone. Both the first black African country to gain independence from colonial rule, Ghana, and the last to be liberated from white racism, South Africa, will appear in historical perspective as part of the contributions of British imperialism and its legacy in the African continent. As a fundamental factor in the African/Afro-American Connection, the English language will remain part of the global equation in which world economic development interplays with culture. The Industrial Revolution was led by English-speaking England, whose leadership, not coincidentally, can be traced in the slave trade, in the abolitionist movement, and in the colonization of Africa.

The world economy is still primarily dominated by an English-speaking country, but this time it is the United States. The World Bank and the International Monetary System are in Washington, D.C.; headquarters of the United Nations are in New York. The leading banking systems are in London and in New York and other American cities. The dominant power in the world economy announces its preferences in the English language. Thus, the African/Afro-American Connection has had to respond to the historic role of the English language, against the background of both the trans-Atlantic slave trade and the partitioning of Africa by European powers.

Black Fate and Africa's Resources

The imperial or territorial imperative in the West's relationship with Africa coincided with the beginnings of the imperative of Africa's resources, though the latter imperative outlasted direct European colonialism in Africa. Throughout much of the nineteenth century there was a good deal of speculation about Africa's "abounding wealth," but this speculative interest was for a while not matched by any determined attempt to prospect for resources in Africa or exploit them.

Africa's agricultural potentialities were realized quite early, but they also were basically underutilized. As a writer put it in 1879, Africa contained "millions of square miles of rich and fertile lands, some of which are open and parklike in their appearance; and others covered with extensive forests of valuable timber, where the sound of the woodman's axe has never yet been heard, and which only require the culture of the husbandman to make them produce an ample return for labor."[3]

Fortunately or unfortunately, fertile land was accompanied in many places by harsh climate for the European. The mosquito and the tse-tse fly took their toll. West Africa, for example, was spared large-scale European settlement partly because its climate was uncongenial to European immigrants and because the mosquito threatened death and devastation to all comers.

It was in the last quarter of the nineteenth century that an entirely new potential source of wealth began to be taken very seriously among Africa watchers.

> By 1875, the discovery of diamonds in South Africa had provided a striking indication of the entirely unexpected riches to be found in Africa, and given new meaning to the wise remark made by Samuel Parchas more than 200 years earlier: "And yet may Africa have a Prerogative in Rarities, and some seeming incredibilities be true."[4]

The possibility of large-scale mineral resources in Africa activated not only a new interest. It also added impetus to the consolidation of territorial annexation and gave impetus to white immigration in southern Africa. The stage was being set for the peculiarly intractable programs of southern Africa, linking economic, strategic, and racial issues with future consequences for American policy toward Africa.

For much of the twentieth century the proportion of Western investment in southern Africa has increased, sometimes substantially exceeding the total invested in the rest of black Africa. Africa as a whole has accounted for 90 percent of the non-Communist world's diamonds, 60 percent of its gold, 40 percent of its cobalt, 34 percent of its bauxite, and nearly 30 percent of its uranium. In turn, the United States has imported 98 percent of its manganese from the outside world, 40 percent of which has come from Africa. The United States also has needed large amounts of chrome from southern Africa, as well as large amounts of cobalt from Zaire.

As indicated previously, the abounding wealth of southern Africa was the major reason that whites immigrated in large numbers into that subregion. The prosperity which emanated from these resources and from white skills then contributed to the intransigence of whites and their desperate effort to maintain white minority rule.

The United States initially adopted the policy of benign neglect toward southern Africa. The status quo seemed to Washington's policy makers more reassuring than the prospect of black majority rule. It was not until the Portuguese empire collapsed in the wake of the Lisbon coup of 1974 that Washington began to take renewed interest in the possibility of change in southern Africa. The penetration, by Cuba and the Soviet Union into Angola from the end of 1975 onward convinced Washington that East-West competition had found a new stage. Henry Kissinger began to contemplate possible shuttle diplomacy in southern Africa.

In the decolonization of the rest of Africa, from Ghana's independence onward, the United States was a relatively minor factor. But in the decolonization and liberation of southern Africa, the United States has become an important actor. Why has the diplomacy of African liberation become partly Americanized in the southern subregion of the African continent?

One reason is that East-West competition has arrived in southern Africa. A second is that London has declined as an influence in the African continent, leaving what Washington regards as a vacuum from the point of view of Western interests. Third, following the withdrawal of Portugal as a colonial power in southern Africa, this so-called vacuum was seen as particularly dangerous. A fourth reason is that southern Africa is of sheer strategic importance, with the Cape serving as one of the great crossroads of world commerce. The United States would thus seek to ensure that the Cape route was in safe hands. A fifth reason for greater American involvement in southern Africa is the fear of a large-scale racial war, which could cause pressures in the domestic politics of the United States and of its own allies. The nightmare of sending in American troops, even as peacemakers, into southern Africa in the style of Lebanon, raises the spector of racial tensions within the American armed forces themselves and within the wider racial scene in the United States. Also fundamental in American calculations is the mineral wealth of southern Africa and its relevance for industrial development in the Western world as a whole. If the strategic industrial minerals of the subregion fell into the wrong hands and were used to threaten industrial strangulation of the Western world, the situation could be almost as explosive for world peace as the situation in the Middle East.

But from the point of view of the African/Afro-American Connection, the issue of southern Africa serves additional functions. In South Africa and Namibia especially, the situation is so racial that it evokes comparison with the black predicament in the United States, which helps maintain a certain level of minimum solidarity between politically conscious Afro-Americans and Africans. The issue of South Africa and apartheid provides additional impetus for such Afro-American organizations as TransAfrica with lobbying interests on Capitol Hill and in Washington generally. The debate about divestment by firms dealing with South Africa also helps to keep Africa as a whole on the agenda of social and political activism in the United States.

The issue of southern Africa also helps to reveal the basic weakness of the Afro-American predicament within the United States. A glaring contrast emerges between the modest impact of black Americans on American policy toward southern Africa and the impressive impact of Jewish Americans on American policy toward the Middle East. Washington's response to the needs of Israel has ranged from a declaration of nuclear alert in defense of Israel in 1973 to the almost indiscriminate showering of millions of dollars every year toward Israel's security and independence. And even with Jews outside Israel, Washington has often shown an active protective concern. The Senate of the United States has been known to vote almost unanimously to withhold most-favored-nation status from the Soviet Union on the grounds that the Soviet Union did not permit its Jewish citizens to emigrate. And yet the same Senate knows quite well, or ought to know, that the blacks of Johannesburg cannot even move from one part of the city to another without risking a confrontation with the pass laws of South Africa. Freedom of movement for Jews in the Soviet Union strikes a more responsive chord in American political institutions than freedom of any kind for blacks of South Africa. One important difference is the comparative effectiveness of the pro-Jewish lobby as against the absolute weakness of the pro-African lobby.

Afro-Americans outnumber Jewish Americans by more than four to one. Indeed, there are twice as many Afro-Americans as there are Jews in the whole world, including the Jews of Israel. And yet the impact of black Americans on American policy toward southern Africa, or indeed toward any other part of the black world, is only a fraction of the impact of Jewish Americans on American policy toward Israel and toward persecuted Jews anywhere else in the world.

It is also worth noting that the parallel of the black American racial experience in relation to apartheid may be carried too far. There is widespread consensus in Africa that the civil rights solution would not work in South Africa and that Andrew Young was, for once, naive in thinking that a civil rights movement within South Africa was what was needed to break the back of apartheid. On the evidence so far, it would seem that nothing but armed stuggle or a major social revolution within South Africa would ever induce the white *minority* régime to give up power to the black majority. In the United States, whites could be relatively "generous" during the civil rights movement without losing power, since they were in the majority. In South Africa, the concession of universal suffrage to blacks would mean the end of white rule and would, therefore, be resisted by whites by fair means or foul.

But while the condition of black people in South Africa is by no means identical with the predicament of blacks in the United States, the shared experience of racial discrimination and, indeed, racial segregation goes toward making black South Africans the closest Africans to black Americans in empathy and a sense of being kindred spirits. Black Americans and black South Africans are probably the two groups of blacks that have suffered the most, historically, from the racial arrogance of white people. The political economy of mineral resources provided part of the setting for racism in southern Africa; the political economy of labor provided the setting of racism in the United States.

Blacks as Actors in the World Economy

The emerging phase in the interaction between the world economy and the black world witnesses Africans and Afro-Americans as actors in the world economy rather than mere cogs in the world machine, as subjects in the economic process rather than mere objects of other people's economic activities. It is indeed true that black labor was once crucial to the total trans-Atlantic exchange, but the labor was not voluntary; it was slave labor under order. Similarly, African land and resources have been a significant feature of the unequal exchange in the global system, but the resources were not subject to African control, and the lands were subject to foreign jurisdiction. What is beginning to happen as a result of the civil rights movement in the United States, on one side, and the anticolonial struggle in Africa, on the other, is the slow emergence of black people as modest decision makers in the global system, blacks as participants in large-scale investment and large-scale trade, and blacks as active members rather than passive objects of global economic processes. The change so far is only modest, but it could be a wave of the future.

Marcus Garvey, the black nationalist from Jamaica who captured the imagination of Americans earlier this century, did attempt to lay the foundations for the black economic empire, parallel to the white-dominated capitalist system but with a considerable autonomy of its own. Marcus Garvey, in fact, believed in black capitalism, and sought ways by which blacks could tap the benefits of capitalism. But many of his adventures ended in tragedy, because Garvey and his movement had capitalist ambition without capitalist efficiency.

The *Black Star* Steamship Line was particularly illustrative of this gap between ambition and efficient performance. The steamship company was capitalized at $10 million. All the ships were named for noted blacks. But the *SS Frederick Douglass*, bought for $165,000, ended up as junk at $1,600. The *SS Antonio Maceo*, formerly the personal yacht of an American millionnaire, cost $160,000, with an additional $25,000 for refitting. It collapsed into pieces off the coast of Cuba. Then there was the *SS Phillis Wheatley*, which sank in the Hudson

River in New York. There was a fourth vessel, which was seized because of nonpayment of debts. Behind many of the enterprises was bad management and sometimes sheer dishonesty.[5]

In the 1970s Idi Amin in Uganda also attempted to release the entrepreneurial energies of black people in his own country. He expelled the Asian businessmen of Uganda, raising once again the issue of whether blacks could be independent economic actors and even economic innovators. Aside from exerting a policy of outrageous oppression against Ugandans, Idi Amin, like Marcus Garvey, also experienced the gap between ambition and performance and witnessed capitalist ambition collapsing on the rocks of black inefficiency.

Nigeria, the largest black nation by far, with a population of 80 to 100 million people, shows similar signs of inefficiency. But because of its size and of its fluctuating resource of oil, Nigeria may lead the way in this phase of African activism within the world economy.

During the course of the 1970s, Nigeria's economic relations with the United States were deepening while its political relations with the United States were, for a while, deteriorating. The deepening economic relations were primarily due to the growing importance of Nigeria as a source of oil for the United States. In 1974, the United States' current account balance-of-payments deficit with Nigeria was $3 billion, the same amount as the United States' worldwide balance-of-trade deficit. In 1976, there was a $5 billion deficit in U.S. balance of payments with Nigeria. By the end of the decade, the deficit had doubled.

In political relations between the two countries, on the other hand, this same period witnessed moments of deterioration. Some of these factors were episodic, while others were structural. The episodic factors included American ambivalence over the Nigerian civil war from 1967 to 1970. Was the United States in favor of one Nigeria, or was there a predisposition toward Biafra?

Another episode was Nixon's snub of Nigerian head of state, Yakubu Gowon, on his visit to the United States in 1974. Nixon and his advisors mucked around with the timetable for the meeting between the two heads of state and offended the Nigerians, who were subordinated to some other claim on President Nixon's time.

In 1974 Nixon resigned, and in 1975 Gowon was overthrown in a military coup in Lagos. In 1976 Gowon's successor, Murtala Muhammed, was assassinated in a traffic jam in Lagos. Was there a British involvement in the assassination of this important Nigerian? Was there some support from the U.S. Central Intelligence Agency? The suspicions cast an additional shadow on relations between Nigeria and the United States.

Then there was the disagreement between Henry Kissinger and Nigeria over the Angolan civil war, especially during the period from 1975 to 1976. In the final analysis, Nigeria decided to side with the Popular Movement for the Liberation of Angola as the legitimate government of the newly liberated Portuguese colony, while Kissinger was attempting to create a constituency of success for the non-Marxist actors in Angola.

In addition to these episodic factors in relations between Nigeria and the United States, there were structural factors. Nigeria was, after all, the largest country by far in Africa, and American policies toward other parts of Africa required some consultation with Lagos.

Nigeria's oil was also part of the structural relations between the United States and Africa. It demanded greater American sensitivity to Lagos as an element in American policy formation for the African continent.

Then there are the ambivalent attitudes toward capitalism in Nigeria. On the one hand, there seems to be little doubt that the capitalist ethos in Nigeria is likely to survive for the rest of the century. On the other hand, Nigerian capitalism is becoming, to some extent, indigenized. For example, American investments in Nigeria decreased when a substantial proportion of equity ownership of oil firms was transferred from American companies to the federal government of Nigeria. There was also legislation to ensure Nigerian majority share in major companies. This has meant a rise of Nigerian capitalism alongside a decline of Western control.

The future of Nigerian capitalism is relatively assured, in spite of the vagaries of the oil market. The country continues to have a vigorous level of individualism. It also continues to manifest a highly developed acquisitive culture. Nigerians are by no means merely target workers ready to go back to the villages after they have acquired enough money to purchase a bicycle or a radio. The Nigerian population has manifested a strong inclination toward cumulative acquisition.

Then there is Nigeria's underlying attachment to liberal values, through competitive party politics and federalism. Sometimes the party politics capitulate to military control, but on the whole, the liberal tendency continues to be strong in Nigeria, even when the soldiers are in power. And the liberal tendency has economic consequences, including a propensity toward capitalism.

The liberal tendency also embodies structural pluralism in the society, diversity of power centers ethnically, regionally, and in terms of religious differentiation. Pluralism, once again, is congenial to the competitive spirit of both capitalism and liberalism.

The Nigerian actor in the world economy is, therefore, part of the emerging new phase in the interplay between the world economy and the black world. Sometimes the Nigerian factor can be active through a deliberately chosen area of inaction. For example, Nigeria did not join the Arab oil embargo of the United States in 1973. As an observer put it: "Had Nigeria joined the Arab oil embargo in 1973–1974, the economic consequences for the United States would have been serious indeed."[6]

What about black America as a participant in the world economy? Of course, black America is already affected by fluctuations in the world economy. Global inflation and the Western recession could cause widespread unemployment among black Americans, who continue to be among the victims of major shifts in the performance of the world economy. But in the last two or three decades black Americans also seem to be on the verge of becoming actors rather than mere cogs in the global system, subjects rather than mere passive objects in the global scheme of things.

But in their relations with the rest of the black world, Afro-Americans are caught up in the contradiction of their location. They, as a group, are among the oppressed of the world; but the United States, as a country, is among the privileged on earth. What does this do to the status of Afro-Americans? They are an oppressed minority in a privileged society. When they travel abroad are Afro-Americans primarily members of the oppressed minority or are they essentially citizens of the privileged society?

This dilemma is more immediately marked between black Americans and Caribbean blacks. The nearness of the United States to the Caribbean could, for blacks, have created a basis of special Pan-African solidarity. But, in fact, the geographic nearness of the two groups is sometimes neutralized by the economic distance between them. The shared geographic hemisphere—the two Americas—has to be balanced against the divided economic hemisphere—the cleavage between the North and the South.

Caribbean blacks sometimes wonder whether American blacks are Americans first and blacks second. When they are at home, American blacks see themselves as blacks first. But when they are abroad do they often perceive themselves as Americans first?

Underlying it all is the contradiction between the United States as an imperialist power, on the one hand, and black Americans as a disadvantaged minority on the other. Yet, in that very contradiction lie the potentialities of black Americans as major actors in the world economy. Their impact on that economy is still modest, but the potentialities are considerable. The unfolding new phase in relationships between the world economy and the black world may have at its center not even merely South Africans as future citizens of the richest black African country, but also Afro-Americans as crucial bridges between the historical predicament of the black world and the continuing dynamism of the world economy.

I have attempted to trace in this essay the four phases of interaction between the world economy and the condition of black peoples across several centuries. Several questions have become apparent. By the second half of the twentieth century are blacks emerging from the shackles of manipulation to the openness of economic initiative? Are they emerging from the bondage of imitation to the freedom of innovation? Will they be sensitized to the needs of the black condition without losing the pragmatism of a new black assertiveness?

The African presence on the world stage is beginning to discipline itself, and its prospects in the economic empire of the future may well depend on a working, productive relationship within the African/ Afro-American Connection.

NOTES

1. A number of scholars have participated in the great debate concerning the numerical scale of the trans-Atlantic slave trade. Such scholars include Philip Curtin and Godfrey Uzoigwe. In this paper we are using the estimations of Roland Oliver and J. D. Fage, *A Short History of Africa* (New York: Penguin Books), 122.
2. For those who did not see the film, E. T. is the central title character from outer space who finds himself on planet earth, left behind by the space ship. When E. T. discovers the telephone device which humans use in communicating with each other between long distances, he stumbles on the idea of telephoning his own home. He is subsequently rescued, and leaves planet earth on his way to his equivalent of "Liberia." The film was entitled, *E. T. The Extra-terrestrial.*
3. John E. Flint, ed., *The Cambridge History of Africa, 1790–1870,* vol. 5 (London, New York, and Melbourne: Cambridge University Press, 1976), 486.
4. *Ibid.,* 487.
5. George Padmore was instructive on these experiments in his book, *Pan-Africanism or Communism? The Coming Struggle for Africa* (London: D. Dobson, 1956).
6. William Jones, "Search for an AID Policy," in *Africa: From Mystery to Maze,* ed. Helen Kitchen (Lexington, Mass.: Lexington Books, 1976), 379.

Response

Davidson Nicol

D R. Mazrui's paper outlined in a lucid and dramatic manner various phases of African/Afro-American policy and their relationship to a larger global system. It may suffice for this paper to enlarge upon a few suggested points after commenting briefly on Mazrui's paper itself. I will begin by noting a few historical facts, some of which were covered by Dr. Skinner concerning Afro-American mercantile enterprises in Africa.

Three figures in the nineteenth century were outstanding as products of the African diaspora, first rising to some eminence in their new countries in the United States and the Caribbean before deciding to return to Africa with concrete plans for economic development: they were Paul Cuffee, Martin Delany, and Robert Campbell.

Paul Cuffee of New Bedford was of African and American Indian ancestry. He had a lively interest in education and was, in addition, successful as a merchant and sailor. He visited Sierra Leone in 1812 and later went back with some Afro-American families as colonists, who no doubt became absorbed eventually into the local population.

Similarly, Martin Delaney, a black physician, with his West Indian partner, Robert Campbell, visited Abeokuta in present-day Nigeria and tried to establish commerce and industry in that city, which was then the center for Western education in the region. These examples are well authenticated in the literature by scholars such as Peter Duignan and Lewis H. Gann and in their own letters and diaries.[1]

There are others as well, for example, Alexander Crummell, an Episcopalian clergyman who spent many years working in education in Liberia before retiring to build and administer St. Luke's Church in Washington, D.C. He also led a black intellectual renaissance movement which culminated in the formation of the Negro Academy.

54

Edward Wilmot Blyden of the Virgin Islands and the United States was perhaps the most well-known because he settled and worked in Liberia, Sierra Leone, and Nigeria, spending the rest of his life in Africa as an educator, politician, and philosopher.

The twentieth century was noted for figures like Marcus Garvey, a Jamaican whose determination and courage in founding the Universal Negro Improvement Association in New York for the opening of shipping and commerce to Africa received due recognition only after his death. He was persecuted during his lifetime and imprisoned. His memory and work for many years remained recognized only in Jamaica, Liberia, and in Limon, Costa Rica, where a large building is still devoted to educational and vocational classes for blacks. He is now remembered with honor in African and American circles.

W. E. B. Du Bois was noted in the United States for his work with the NAACP and his editorship of *Crisis* and worldwide for his work with the Pan-African movement. He ended his days in Ghana in 1963 as editor of the *Encyclopedia Africana*.

An outstanding repatriate of the African diaspora in the twentieth century was Felix Eboué from French Guyana. Other French colonies in the New World were in Canada and Louisiana on the American mainland, and on Haiti, Martinique, and Guadeloupe in the Caribbean islands, where the African element was largest. Eboué joined the French Colonial Service, and with competence and skill he rose during the 1939–1945 war to be governor-general of French Equatorial Africa, giving much-needed support to General de Gaulle of the Fighting French troops, a move which later played a key role in the liberation of occupied Europe.

In the commercial field in recent years, Percy Sutton, former president of the borough of Manhattan in New York and a successful black entrepreneur, has used modern methods for strengthening the African/Afro-American Connection. Instead of emigrating to Africa, he and his black associates and family have traveled to Nigeria regularly to introduce and establish business concerns related to communications.

There are, in addition, an increasing number of Afro-American men and women in this century who, in their individual capacities or as officials of the U.S. government, corporations, or church groups, or even as officials of local African governments and universities, have given and continue to give outstanding, sometimes unacknowledged, service to African aspirations and progress. They are content to have had the opportunity to make their own unique contribution to the land of their ancestors. The Afro-American figures have had visions of economic and educational development for the continent of Africa, which have been met with varying degrees of success.

Economic Power

As Africans acquire more economic power, so do Afro-Americans. Economic power is of much importance in international politics. Nigeria, for example, was able to refuse the visit of a powerful U.S. secretary of state and to challenge a European secretary of state by nationalizing a major oil company from that country in reprisal for an unfavorable political action in South Africa. Only its economic power and independence could have given Nigeria the strength to face great powers on such combative terms.

In the United States, the important work of the Congressional Black Caucus and TransAfrica in Washington, D.C., have made a significant impact on African development, on the provision of U.S. aid to the continent, and in the fight against apartheid and racial discrimination in South Africa. Their work in providing effective lobbies at the seat of legislative power in the economically most powerful nation in the world is of central importance. The Jewish community has shown how effective lobbying can be in gaining support for Israel, the home of their own ancestors, and this has encouraged Afro-Americans to attempt the same for Africa.

Dis-Africanization

Attention has been given to the dis-Africanization of blacks in American society—individuals of African ancestry are called *black Americans* instead of *Afro-* or *African-Americans* in acknowledgment of their country of origin. There might be a problem here, but it is not insurmountable. The description *Euro-Americans* or *European-Americans* is not used, so why *Afro-American* or *African-American*? The answer is that when the ancestors of Afro-Americans and Afro-Caribbeans left Africa, involuntarily or voluntarily, there were no demarcated nation-states such as those in Europe and Asia—Italy, Ireland, Poland, Greece, China, and Japan. In addition, the immigrant communities from Europe and Asia, on arriving in the United States, kept together identifiably and were not fragmented by slavery and forced internal migration. Thus, they could be described as Italian-American, Irish-American, Polish-American, Greek-American, Chinese-American, and Japanese-American, for example, but with blacks, only the continental description of *African-American* or *Afro-American* was possible.

In Brazil, where black communities were kept together, there are still discernibly Angolan, Yoruba, and Hausa groups. This is also the case with some Caribbean islands like Cariaccou, where, in the Big Drum Dance, various African communities display their origin as

Temne, Ibo, and so on. In Cuba, likewise, Yoruba, Calabar, and Ibo societies may sometimes be discerned.

The question of pinpointing correctly one's place of origin and so establishing an identity is of greater emotional importance to citizens of the African diaspora than present-day citizens of nation-states in Africa realize. This partially accounts for the popularity of Alex Haley's book *Roots,* in which by careful historical and oral research he established his African ancestor as an eighteenth-century kidnap victim from a village in the present-day republic of Gambia.[2]

Another anomaly in the Africanization of Afro-Americans is that the term *black* has ceased to be descriptive or accurate, since a significant proportion of the group is not black in color and some are minimally black in ancestry. The term has now become both cultural and political. A white man who won an election in Stockton, California, by describing himself as black has been challenged in court by his defeated opponent, who claims that the victor is a white man and not a black one and so had won his election by fraud and misrepresentation to a predominantly black electorate. The terms *African-American* and *Afro-American* are useful in covering a multitude of genetic strains and colors. The Organization of African Unity— the bottom line in matters African—has white Tunisians, brown Egyptians, and black Kenyans and Tanzanians. *Black* will, however, continue to be used for some time to describe Afro-Americans, as a differentiation from *white.*

Educational Institutions

The role of Afro-American educational institutions in African political development, especially in the first half of the twentieth century, was of considerable importance. Relatively small black institutions such as Lincoln University in Pennsylvania and others such as Howard, Fisk, Tuskegee, Hampton, and Wilberforce universities produced more African political leaders than the major American and European universities. In his book, *Black Nationalism,* Professor Essien-Udom points out the importance of black churches and institutions, confirmed by the autobiographies of great Africans such as Azikiwe of Nigeria, Nkrumah of Ghana, and Hastings Banda of Malawi.[3]

Slavery and Abolition

In his paper Dr. Ali Mazrui stated that "in time, the black races were relegated to the lowest level of human stratification." This statement may need some qualification, for although this may have been so in Europe, in China the white races were the ones relegated to the lowest level of civilization. Perhaps the Chinese had not yet met blacks. Nevertheless, in the fifteenth, sixteenth, and seventeenth centuries, black chiefs and kings were addressed as equals by European monarchs, whose ambassadors in Africa stooped and bowed low to African kings and nobles, as Africans were later asked to do to European officials.

In North Africa, white European Christians, like Cervantes, the author of *Don Quixote*, were sold into slavery, and white women slaves were to be found in the harems of North African monarchs and noblemen. Black, mixed, and white merchants all participated in the sale of black men and women into slavery. There were numerical differences in the trade, but racial discrimination should not be blamed for slavery's immorality and wickedness.

But an important fact seldom found in the literature is that, in equal measure, African chiefs (the Temne regent Naimbana of Sierra Leone and later Saro) and Sierra Leonean-Nigerians (Bishop Crowther of the Niger and Superintendent Isaac Willoughby of Lagos) put forth as much effort in their own way toward the abolition of slavery as did the European humanitarians (Sharp, Wilberforce, and Clarkson) and the U.S. abolitionists (Lincoln, Lewis Tappan, and Gerrit Smith). Even though the numbers of anti-slavery forces were smaller in Africa, slavery could not have been completely abolished without the cooperative efforts of Africans, Afro-Americans, and Afro-Caribbeans. The African abolitionists sometimes suffered more because their whole economy was based on slavery, and they did not have an alternative as did the European and American abolitionists. Their efforts should not, however, be minimized or misinterpreted.

Repatriates

The reasons for repatriation to Africa have been rightly pointed out to be humanitarian, but in some cases they were admittedly racist. Free black men were a drain on the economy of late eighteenth-century London and so were shipped to Sierra Leone in 1787. Free Afro-Americans who had fought in the American War for Independence on the side of the British were denied promised land in Nova Scotia on racist grounds and so were also shipped to Sierra Leone in 1792. Maroons from Jamaica were a threat to white plantation owners and were thus kidnapped by trickery in 1796 and sent to Nova Scotia in 1800. They were also sent to Sierra Leone. (The present-day Maroons in remote villages in the mountains of Jamaica and the black Americans in Nova Scotia still remember these incidents in their oral traditions.) Free

Afro-Americans were judged to be potential or actual sources of dis-affection among those still enslaved in nineteenth-century America and were urged and helped to return to Liberia.

In addition to all these groups, there were the recaptives from the slave ships, who after the abolition of slavery and the slave trade were freed by European and American warships and taken to Sierra Leone and Liberia. These recaptives became the ancestors chiefly of the large majority of the present-day Creoles of Sierra Leone, the Congo people of Liberia, and the original Christians of Abeokuta. They were Westernized by the original black settlers and missionaries, white and black, from Europe and America. They also were settled in other areas, such as Banjul in Gambia, St. Helena, Ascension Island, and Fernando Po in Equatorial Guinea. Many of them took on Euro-pean names either at Christian baptism as part of their Westernization or, in sheer weariness, at the constant mispronunciation or misuse of their African names.

English and the African Diaspora

The importance of English as the language in which the main con-cepts of permanent power in the world economy announces it prefer-ences has been stressed. The natives of Britain now form a minority of those who speak English: over a billion people in India, America, and the Commonwealth also speak English. It still remains perhaps one of the greatest gifts Britain has given world civilization and, indeed, world peace. Many communities in Commonwealth African countries and in the United States and India would not be able to understand each other and form manageable nation-states without the help of the English language. Nevertheless, English-speaking Af-ricans owe it to African unity to acquire another European language (French, Portuguese, or Spanish) and Arabic—all languages that are similar to English in their degree of influence—if they are to communi-cate with neighboring African countries. Ideally, acquiring an African language in addition to their own would help to forge unity within their respective countries. Transnational languages such as Swahili, Lingala, Hausa, and Krio can be useful in intra-African transnational communication. Afro-Americans start with a great advantage in Africa if they can speak an African language.

Ambition vs. Inefficiency

Black inefficiency is often mentioned in discussions of African de-velopment. Inefficiency is due to lack of training and lack of professional and managerial skills. A change of attitude can be engendered in Africans with leadership potential by instilling concepts of planning for the future.

Other factors that play a part in fostering inefficiency are undernutrition, malnutrition, and debilitating diseases. In addition, both the tropical climate and the instrinsic physiology of the rhythm of sleep centers produce low productivity in the afternoon, which constitutes half the working day in Africa, as inherited from the colonial pattern imposed from northern Europe. The Mediterranean peoples such as the Spanish, Portuguese, and Italians are much more logical and sensible in their working hours: they leave the afternoons free and take up work again later in the afternoon and early evening. Reorganization of work periods may lessen seeming African inefficiency and increase productivity.

Black inefficiency can be vigorously removed only by black leaders because its existence, although deplored, is still tacitly accepted by foreigners as intrinsic and thus not eliminated because it provides an excuse for denying leadership to blacks and for increasing their dependence on foreigners. On the other hand, black efficiency and leadership have been recognized by forward-looking transnational corporations as being both desirable politically and beneficial economically. African governments have made it clear also that the continued local existence of these companies depends on sharing with Africans and developing the latter's managerial skills toward the Africanization of the company's professional, technical, and in some cases, senior management staff—levels which were formerly dominated by foreigners. The rapid progress of Afro-American business in the United States recorded by magazines such as *Black Enterprise, Essence,* and *Ebony* offers an opportunity for exporting these skills to Africa without the innate racial bias present in some, although decidedly not all, foreigners working in Africa.

Nigeria and the United States

A large final question raised is the tension between Nigeria, the largest African country, and the government of the United States. This problem is surmountable, and it is in the interest of both countries to resolve it quickly. Nigeria is troubled by the complacency, or sometimes outright support, it feels some Western European countries and the United States are giving South Africa and its policy of legal, racial discrimination and oppression of its black population.

The Soviet Union and the People's Republic of China support African protest at the United Nations, but it is patronizing to African states for

Western countries to regard African protest as being communist-inspired. Black Africa knows that it cannot expect the West to take armed action against South Africa, but neither does it expect the West to actively arm South Africa. The divestiture procedures against South Africa which forward-looking states such as Connecticut and New York are now taking (added to the activities of churches and universities in Europe and the United States against South African racist policies) should be reassuring to Nigeria and other African countries. They offer yet another avenue for participation which Afro-Americans can vigorously pursue to promote peaceful democratic rule in an African continent where all races can live productively and in harmony and safety.

NOTES

1. See Peter Duignan and Lewis H. Gann, *The United States and Africa: A History* (Cambridge University Press, 1984) for a comprehensive treatment.
2. Alex Haley, *Roots, The Saga of an American Family* (Garden City: Doubleday, 1976).
3. E. U. Essien-Udom, *Black Nationalism, A Search for an Identity in America* (Chicago: University of Chicago Press, 1967).

The Liberian Experience: A Personal Analysis

Augustus F. Caine

THE Liberian Experience is something that is very difficult to be dispassionate about. Even Liberian scholars differ in their opinions of the experience, depending on their own perspective, and depending particularly on their position in the system that we have developed in this country. Because of the shortage of time, I would like to summarize my experience simply by saying that one can explain the Liberian Experience in terms of what I call a *dominant-minority relationship*. This is a concept which means that in a community, one group, regardless of its numerical strength, exercises power and control over all others. This is the essence of the Liberian Experience.

To document this, one must look at the various institutional segments of Liberian life. Let us take political life first. I think if one reads the accounts of this country he will see that we had a dual administration—an interior administration and a coastal administration. The coastal administration was administered according to the norms of the West as brought here by the settlers. In the interior, we had what we call *customary laws*, based upon the customs and traditions of the people. Those customs were upheld only if they were not "repugnant" to the introduced laws—the laws that came from abroad. The people in the interior could vote, but they were not represented in the legislature initially. There were differences in the way the law treated these two groups of people. If an individual was from the interior, he was regarded as an "uncivilized man"—or any other words you can fashion or think about.

The legal system operated to make a distinction between people in the interior and people on the littoral. And we must keep in mind the concept of *repugnance*. There were what were called then a *first-class citizenship* and a *second-class citizenship*. The first-class citizenship, of course, was here on the coast, and the second-class citizenship was in the interior of the country, where so-called tribesmen lived. We did not refer to any citizenship as second class, but our status was implicit in the way the country was administered. We can say representatives of the central government in Monrovia were sent out to the interior to see to it that things were administered according to what was desired in Monrovia. These two types of citizenship—first-class and second-class—were evidences of the dominance of the minority living in Monrovia.

Let us look at the economy. The people on the coast, for various reasons, occupied the commanding positions in the Liberian economy. If we look at the public service, the evidence is plain. If we look at the roster of cabinet ministers, over say a century, it would be possible to document this in terms of the overrepresentation of the settler population among cabinet positions—people in positions of authority and power. If we look at the private sector, particularly in this century, we will also see that. And I am addressing myself here especially to the time of President Tolbert, when a prevailing concept was that the government and the private industries and corporations were in a partnership. Companies like LAMCO, Firestone, and Bong Mines—these organizations or agencies were the ones, except for Firestone, with which the government was in partnership. The effect of this was that when one wanted to "Liberianize" a position in the private sector, the government of Liberia took a strong hand in making that replacement. And I think that, according to the evidence, we will see plainly that the president of Liberia took his own men and put them there, and usually, I think, they were people of the settler community.

Let us look at the military. We did not have military establishments in this country until about 1908, I think. There was the question of whether or not Liberia had power and authority over the areas of the country that it claimed. Before 1900, colonial powers really did not recognize our authority over these areas. Adopting a concept of "effective control," we began to send military personnel along the boundaries with these colonial powers' territories, to help guard them because we wanted to show that we were in control of these areas. So in 1908, this military occupation was institutionalized in what was called the "Frontier Force." Soldiers were taught one principle: "order be order." It meant a soldier must do what he was told regardless of the reason. Tennyson said, "Theirs is not to reason why, theirs is but to do and die." The Liberian soldiers were socialized according to this precept. Now, if a soldier were so trained, the government could use him to do anything, even against the people of the country. There is evidence that the soldiers were used against the people of the country. So that the military served not actually to preserve the security of the state, at least not primarily, but rather to protect particular functionaries and to keep their régimes from falling.

Take education. Due to the lack of funds, the government was not able to spread educational opportunities throughout the country. But as far back as the early part of this century, say 1910 or there about, we placed on the books a compulsory education law. I take this to mean that the government was interested in seeing to it that people went to school. But, as I said, because of the lack of funds, it was not possible to implement this law.

Now, in the Tubman administration, with its "Open-Door Policy," many investors came to Liberia, and the government's income increased. As a result, the government did spread educational opportunity throughout the country, and access to education became available to many more people. A scholarship program was established, not by President Tubman but by President Barclay, between 1940 and 1943 or there about. But President Tubman strengthened that program because, of course, he had the funds. It was in my own little town of Cape Mount that the first group passed through. All of them were settlers, but over time that education program included everybody in this country, so that children of all segments of the population—I mean children from people of all segments of the Liberian population—were able to benefit from it. As a result, today we have something like a technocratic elite, which is composed of people from every segment of the country.

I want to go back a bit to politics again. In 1964, the government of Liberia decided to abolish formally this dual citizenship—first-class and second-class citizenship. It did so by establishing four new counties carved out of what we used to call the interior administration. These counties had status equal to the five on the littoral. They were able to send representatives to the legislature based on their population, and their representatives were accorded the same rights as those here on the coast. However, the people in these counties began to say that they wanted gownsmen and elected them in 1954 at the Cape Palmas Unification Conference. *Gownsman* is a concept which means an illiterate person. The gownsman must represent his people. Even if the people had a Ph.D. who could speak for them in the legislature, they preferred a gownsman. This gownsman was a representative, but he did not represent his people, not really—he did not represent their view, because he was illiterate and could not really perform his role. He spoke through an interpreter. I worked there myself as a journal clerk, so I know what I am talking about. I am not getting it out of a book. And I saw that there was little opportunity for any interpretation. In any case, it would have been very difficult for the legislature to work through interpreters. So, there were practical difficulties confronting the procedure, even if the government did want it.

How the situation has changed, particularly since the Tolbert administration, when one could elect anybody one wanted. There had been tremendous pressures for change in that area. The settler community exercised its interests in this society through the True Whig Party. The True Whig Party, theoretically, was a mass party but, in fact, it was not. It was made up of government officials. Nobody had to apply for membership or take out a membership. One automatically became a member of the True Whig Party upon taking a government job. The government and the party then became very good allies. The government and the party became synonymous. The True Whig Party was really the government of Liberia. If one fought the party, he could not keep his job in the public bureaucracy. And so things went on. This dominance can be observed in every area. If a soldier was imbued with the notion that he must obey, then the government could send him to a man's house to get him out and send him to jail regardless of what he did, because the man ordering the arrest was not asked why. Intelligent obedience was not the norm in which the soldier had been trained. He had been trained to obey. Obedience is better than sacrifice, so the military became an instrument in the hands of the power elite, this dominant minority, in carrying out its purposes in the land.

Now, having said all this, it is also important to say that there is much evidence that individual members of this power elite were well motivated in the past. Some of them brought the aborigine children into their homes and reared them, gave them their names, and actually fostered them. Since the Tubman administration, individual settlers have been interested in particular elements of the aboriginal population, and they have fostered these people.

The question of intermarriage, on which I want to end, apart from the initial color problem that split the settler population into mulattoes and people of darker hue, has not been too much of a problem. In the first century, of course, as I have said, this was difficult because within the settler population there was a conflict of color. Settlers brought here the problem they had over there, and because of that, the settler population was weakened. Color distinctions broke up their ranks, but after a while they coalesced and became one group, vis-à-vis the aboriginal population.

Now, we have just had a change of government in 1980. This shows that not everybody was satisfied with the pace of change. But you know, somebody has told us that revolutions are not brought by those who have nothing and want something, but by those who have something and want more.

Response

Ruth Simms Hamilton

PROFESSOR Augustus Caine argues that it is difficult to be dispassionate about the Liberian experience and that, for Liberian scholars, interpretations vary depending on background, interests, and perspectives. Neither Liberia nor its scholars are unique in this respect. Given the possibilities for varying interpretations and insights, however, it is necessary for Liberian and non-Liberian scholars to present valid data and to place their problems within a meaningful conceptual, historical, and comparative framework to allow for reliable interpretations of the universal and unique aspects of the Liberian experience or some other cultural experience. In this context, one must welcome the honesty and candor presented in Caine's very brief decription of particular aspects of the Liberian experience. If there is a problem with Caine's paper, it is perhaps not so much his effectiveness or his perspective that are at issue, as much as it is the need for greater contextual and conceptual clarity in explaining the sociohistorical dimensions of the Liberian experience. The remainder of this discussion raises some issues pertinent to the analytical and conceptual aspects of the paper.

In discussing the nature of the relationship "between those who came and those who were here," Caine uses the term *dominant-minority relationship*. However, since reference is to a relationship, it is more appropriate to refer to a dominance-subordinance relationship involving a dominant minority (Americo-Liberians) and a subordinate majority (indigenous Liberians). Thus, the *dominance-subordinance* concept can be correctly used to get at the nature of power and control and to take into account the institutional manifestations of inequality, e.g., education, military, government, and legal. It is obvious, for example, that over time Caine sees Liberian political institutions as central to understanding dominance-subordinance relationships within the country. Thus, reference is made to dual administrations in the coastal and interior areas of the country, the use of the military in maintaining order, and the significance of cabinet positions in maintaining inequality and power within a dual administration.

It is unfortunate that Caine ignores the crucial significance of the state in Liberian historical development. The role of the Liberian state in regulating and channeling relationships is so fundamental to his analysis. The ideology, material culture, and conventional wisdom of the state all affect the policies adopted toward the indigenous people, as do the pressures exerted by foreign interests. One unifying concept that can bring some conceptual and historical unity to Caine's paper is the notion of the *state*.[1]

Americo-Liberians and the Liberian State

A working proposition is this: A culturally distinct minority, Americo-Liberians, gained control of Liberia, institutionalized its distinctiveness, and used the state apparatus to acquire and maintain its ascendancy. The guiding principles, therefore, were inequality and political domination. The central political system, the Liberian state, became the basis of settler domination.

In essence, with the imposition of Americo-Liberian settler rule, state apparatuses were created to exercise dominion over indigenous peoples and institutions in the "colony." These minority settlers, similar to the British settlers in Kenya and the Afrikaners and British in South Africa, created a state equipped with bureaucratic-military apparatuses and mechanisms of government which enabled them, through various operations, to subordinate the "native" people.

State apparatuses include the police and military, administrative or executive branches, the legislature, and judiciary. Various institutions, including educational, religious, and cultural, as well as trade unions and political parties, serve the function of reproducing material, ideological, and cultural relations. Among the state apparatuses, most crucial is the role of the government. The point again is that the interests of the Americo-Liberian settlers were represented in the nature of the state and its apparatus and laws.

It is necessary to be critical of the emphasis Caine placed on the Liberian soldier having been imbued with the notion to obey. In the Liberian context, is the real issue whether soldiers obey or "order be order"? For the Liberian soldier, or any other professional soldier, the job is to obey and carry out commands. Is not the critical issue the use of the military as an instrument of state power? Perhaps it would be more useful to analyze the Liberian state as it became equipped with bureaucratic-military apparatuses that enabled the ruling settler elites, through routine operations, to subordinate the autochthonous people. Using such an approach, it is possible to assess the changes over time of the use of the military as part of the state apparatus. Such a comparative historical perspective becomes especially pertinent given the military coup in 1980, which not only changed the course of Liberian history but also inaugurated a state system under the control of the military.

Are Americo-Liberians a Class?

If, as Caine argues, the people on the coast occupied the commanding positions in the Liberian economy, to what extent can they be defined as a class, representing class interests? One thing is clear: the dominant group exercised administrative and military control during the period of capitalist growth in Liberia. The strategic position the state occupied in Liberia allowed the state bourgeoisie, historically Americo-Liberians, to establish a place for itself in the existing relations of production. Two concerns should be important here. First, the state is not only an instrument of political domination but also a source of economic power. Thus, the state can appropriate a large part of the economic surplus and deploy it in bureaucratically directed economic activity in the name of promoting economic development. Second, with its access to power and control, the Liberian bureaucracy may have taken on some of the characteristics of a class, e.g., control of the economic infrastructure and use of it as a means of exploitation and control of the means of repression that included various devices to maintain dominance.[2]

In this context, Caine's reference to government and private corporations and industries in partnership becomes particularly meaningful. Having established a place for themselves in the existing relations of production, did the settlers, acting as a class, use the state to parachute themselves into the private sector at the expense of the indigenous people? Certainly, this is tacit in Caine's paper although never directly addressed. Again, the concept of the *state* can be analytically useful in pursuing the notion of Americo-Liberians as a class formed around the apparatus of the state—a class with an interest quite distinct from and antagonistic to the interests of the masses of indigenous peoples.

Changing Social Relations: Gownsmen and Technocrats

Caine argues that in the mid-sixties, dual administration was abolished in Liberia, giving people of the interior representation to the state legislature. The argument is that the people sent illiterate persons, "gownsmen," to represent them even if highly educated people were available and, one assumes, willing to serve. This, according to Caine, did not represent the interests of the people because of communications and problems of interpretation in the Monrovian-based legislature. Later, he contends that under the Tolbert administration the people could elect anybody they wanted. Something is missing here. Is the contention that certain state administrations were more tolerant of illiterates than others? If so, why? Is it a question of whether a government bureaucracy is able to allow the inclusion of diversified representation regardless of whom the people elect? A more fundamental question is why, under certain conditions, people elect to send a particular type of representative rather than another type? The point Caine is attempting to make is not clear.

One possible approach to clarifying the issues is to begin with the working proposition that ruling groups try to preserve the social order in which their interests are embedded. It is important, therefore, to understand and to make explicit, the conditions under which it is in the interest of those who control the state to give some concession to other groups and/or exploiting classes in order to maintain the cohesion of the society. Historically, political alliances with other sections of an indigenous bourgeoisie created a comprador-like class which acted mainly as an intermediary for colonial states. In Liberia, for instance, under what conditions did the ruling Americo-Liberians move to integrate and make political alliances with "local" (indigenous) elites? Thus, while Caine seems to be critical of the people's decision to send "gownsmen" to represent them, it may well be that they understood the nature of the Liberian state and the possibilities for co-optation.

In another context, Caine maintains that lack of funds prevented the government from implementing compulsory education laws throughout Liberia. However, when funds did become available under the Tolbert adminstration greater educational opportunity was spread through the country. Allegedly, one consequence of this change is that today there exists a "technocratic elite which is composed of people from every segment of the country." Again, Caine makes a giant leap without providing understanding of the process or the nature of inequality, which he posits as so fundamental to the dominance-subordinance relationship. For example, under varying economic conditions, what was the nature of access to opportunity structures? Did Americo-Liberians have disproportionate access to education even when funds were allegedly not available as well as when they were available? Assuming the availability of funds, what were the differences in the quantity and quality of educational opportunities between coastal and interior peoples? Moreover, to understand the significance of an emerging technocratic elite within the historical development of the Liberian sociopolitical structure, it would be important to know (1) the quantity and type of representation of Liberians across all ethnic groups, including the Americo-Liberians; (2) the recency of entry of the various groups into the technocracy; (3) the relative distribution of the diverse ethnic groups in different technocratic levels of expertise and responsibility; and (4) the critical events and points over time which account for these changes, including changes under the Doe administration.

The observations made by Caine, although lacking in analytical and explanatory depth, do represent examples of areas of social and political relations that can provide insight into and understanding of the changing role of the state and the implications for individual and group mobility within Liberia.

Dominance-Subordinance Relations as Process

Professor Caine is successful in making us aware that the sociopolitical history of Liberia has been largely characterized by structural relationships of inequality and domination. Prior to 1980, the dominant group, Americo-Liberians, had disproportionate contol over economic resources, a presumptive privilege in social relations, and a virtual monopoly, until recently, in access to the state. On the other hand, the subordinate group, mainly peoples of the interior, were economically constrained, with little standing in social and political relations, and lacked access to the state. Moreover, the state, as the dominant group's political power center, also had important ideological functions. As Caine notes, the ideological focus was on "uncivilized man" and "repugnance"; this was precisely because of the "uncivilized" or "tribal" nature of what was being controlled. Although Caine is quick to note that individual members of the Americo-Liberian power elite took an interest in the so-called aboriginal children and population, even this kind of attitude and behavior must be clearly and honestly analyzed. Paternalism, in its many forms and historical contexts, has always been associated with the dominant toward the subordinate population. Thus, a full analysis of "settler interest in the aboriginals" must be made within the framework of the overall situation of structural inequality.

Although I have argued for the usefulness of the concept of the *state* as an analytical tool to debunk particular aspects of Liberian sociohistorical development, it is necessary to emphasize that the idea is not to be understood as a static phenomenon. Certainly, the indigenous people of Liberia did not passively accept the oppressive rule of the settler community. For example, even if the concept of *repugnance* was imposed, there is no reason to assume that the people of the interior accepted the "uncivilized" labeling. The concern is how did the people live life as they transformed life? In the struggle for decency and liberation, what mechanisms and strategies did they use, which may have ranged from the content of child-rearing and the sending of "gownsmen" to the legislature, to more direct and overt forms of struggle and protest? Perhaps the ultimate contradiction is personified in the rise to power of Sergeant Doe, the violent deaths of prominent Americo-Liberian leaders, and the symbolic, ideological, and political significance of all that is represented by the current state régime. The Liberian experience is indeed a dialectic, an ongoing situation of conflict and change, a product of historical development within the context of world society.

Finally, study and analysis of the universal and unique aspects of the Liberian experience provide an opportunity for the student of African diaspora studies to gain important comparative insights into the larger diaspora historical development. Caine's use of the concept *dominance-subordinance* to explain inequality in Liberia demonstrates how victims of oppression in the diaspora can themselves use the same techniques to dominate and suppress other black people, whether as settlers in Liberia or Sierra Leone or as a privileged minority in a country such as Haiti. Furthermore, the notion of the *state* as a concept that facilitates understanding of the nature of power and control can be used to analyze the comparative experiences of inequality and domination that appear to be a larger defining characteristic of peoples of the African diaspora. The challenge is to analyze various state systems and policies as they have been used to oppress and generate conflict and change for peoples of the African diaspora, both as numerical minorities in Western industrial nations and as majorities or sizeable minorities in various geopolitical situations. This may extend from the black experience in Israel to the social situations and ongoing historical realities of peoples of African descent in Cuba and Surinam. In all of these instances, as well as Liberia, the importance of race-ethnic-class contradictions must be carefully analyzed in relationship to other ideological, political, cultural, and economic structures and institutions. The search for the patterns and relations as they change over time and under certain conditions must be relentless. Analytical concepts must be employed to facilitate explanations of internal relations of people and nations, as well as the external relations to a larger world system of which they are an integral part and to which so many of the conflicts and contradictions are endemic.

NOTES

1. An interesting discussion of the theory of the state can be well understood in Hamza Alavi, "The State in Post-Colonial Societies—Pakistan and Bangladesh," *New Left Review* 74 (July-August 1972): 59-81.
2. A relevant article on the significance of classes is C. Meillassoux, "A Class Analysis of the Bureaucratic Process in Mali," *The Journal of Development Studies* (January 1970).

Response

Herschelle S. Challenor

"THE Liberian Experience," Professor Augustus Caine's personal analysis, poignantly encapsulates the theme of the seminar, "Dynamics of the African/Afro-American Connection: From Dependency to Self-Reliance." Following 155 years of domination by the Afro-American settler population and those persons incorporated into that group, the indigenous peoples of Liberia revolted against this subordination and opted for greater self-reliance within their own country. However, the aftermath of the revolution of April 12, 1980, has demonstrated that despite the dual administration and de facto dual citizenship referred to by Professor Caine, a degree of interdependence has been established between the two groups, thereby preventing a complete rupture with the past.

Liberia demonstrates the challenges and opportunities of the African/Afro-American encounter. While signaling warnings about the Garveyist solution, it reveals the resiliency of what has become a symbiotic relationship despite its historic inequities. Nevertheless, blacks in the New World should avoid a wholesale return that might lead to a "Liberianization" of Africa. Instead, they should establish sustainable linkages with Africans in which the power relationships are based upon individual achievement, rather than such ascriptive factors as place of birth.

It is noteworthy that the most successful "settler" states are those for which the United Kingdom and, in the case of Liberia, the United States served as the principal mediating authority between the settler population and the host community, i.e., the United States, Canada, Australia, South Africa, and Israel. The two principal examples of French settler societies, Haiti and Algeria, failed following protracted armed struggle. The fate of the remaining territories of Overseas France is uncertain.

74

Settler groups have been most successful in maintaining their preeminence through territorial expansion, through retaining subordination by political and military force, and/or through transforming their minority status into majority status via emigration, incorporation, or removal of the host group.

In many respects the Liberian experience reflects in microcosm the dynamics of the *dependencia* model. Dependency theorists suggest that the historical process of the development and expansion of capitalism has led to both the economic development of the industrial capitalist core states and structural underdevelopment in the dependent peripheral states. Despite its *de jure* independence after 1847, Liberia and its Americo-Liberian ruling elite served as wards of the United States and Great Britain until World War II. During World Wars I and II and the interwar years, Liberia was caught up in what dependency theorists refer to as the world capitalist system as a supplier of rubber and iron ore vital to the war effort. It also served as an important port in the African theater during the wars and became a significant port of registry for commercial shipping.

The Liberian settler class acted as the agents of external commercial and industrial interests and facilitated the exploitation of the host community by these groups. Fanon's critique of the national bourgeoisie that emerged after independence in many developing countries is applicable to the Liberian case. He suggested that this class served as an intermediary,

> because it is bereft of ideas, because it lives to itself and cuts itself off from the people, undermined by its hereditary incapacity to think in terms of all the problems of the nation and seen from the point of view of the whole of that nation, the national middle class will have nothing to do than to take on the role of manager for Western enterprise. . . .[1]

In a real sense, the history of Liberia through the 1980 coup provides a classic example of how the *dependencia* state may collapse, not because of the so-called Marxist contradictions in the transstate capitalist relationships, but rather because of class forces in the peripheral state that hinder the country's development.

Rather than the Americo-Liberian class collapsing under the sheer weight of its repression, it was in part its marginal success in granting greater access to the peoples in the hinterland that led to its demise. In this sense, Professor Caine's closing statement is both appropriate and profound: "revolutions are not brought by those who have nothing and want something, but by those who have something and want more."

Professor Caine skillfully summarizes the extent of the Americo-

Liberian settler hegemony over the indigenous peoples of Liberia. Dominance was established and sustained through a series of political, legal, economic, educational, and social relationships.

Wholesale assimilation of the indigenous peoples into the ranks of the settler community was resisted. However, there were ways by which transition into the so-called honorable group could take place.

In the early years of the colony, Americo-Liberians added to their numbers by encouraging other New World and continental Africans to emigrate. The "Congoes" was a generic name given to those Nigerians, Congolese, and other Africans who had been freed from slave vessels en route to the New World and sent to Liberia. After the election of 1869, when the True Whig Party came to power largely as a result of a division within the Republican Party over skin color and ancestry, the Congoes became important political allies of a lower-class segment of the Americo-Liberian community. It is noteworthy that the April coup singled out not only the Americo-Liberians but also the Congoes.

So-called tribal peoples were incorporated into the Americo-Liberian community by three principal means: (1) the ward system, institutionalized in 1838, whereby a child of a tribal family was raised by a settler family; (2) miscegenation, through liaisons or intermarriage; (3) co-optation, through tribal leaders who had facilitated Americo-Liberian control over their areas. As a reward for their actions, they were able to participate in those benefits available to Americo-Liberians, i.e., salaried posts and education abroad for their children.

After the initial purchase of what is now Montserado County, a stretch of land 130 miles by 40 miles, the settlers expanded territorially through land purchases; establishment of protectorates over and commercial treaties with local ethnic groups, i.e., those of the 1850s negotiated with the Vai, Gola, and Buzi groups; and through the rights of discovery and conquest, as with the Kru and Grebo. The black settlers, like their American counterparts, spoke of their manifest destiny to civilize the peoples of the interior.

Although a Department of the Interior was created in 1868 to better manage the hinterland, it was not until the beginning of the twentieth century that any effective administration was established. The settlers wanted to establish control over the interior principally to ward off British and French territorial ambitions. President Arthur's recognition of the peoples in the hinterland as Liberian citizens during this period was the government's first attempt to accord such status to the non-settler population. It should be noted that a similar distinction between citizens and subjects which existed in French colonial Africa, whereby citizenship was granted only to metropolitan French, mulattoes, and

Africans born in the four communes of Senegal, was not ended until after World War II.

The low point in Americo-Liberian and host community relations occurred during the administration of Charles D. B. King, between 1920 and 1930. King and his vice-president, Allen N. Yancy, had to resign following a League of Nations indictment of several top Liberian officials on charges of domestic slavery, abuse of forced labor, and unjust labor-recruitment policies. President Edwin Barclay succeeded King. Although Barclay outlawed domestic slavery and the export of contract labor and reorganized the interior administrations to make local officials more responsible for their transgressions, he took retaliatory action against political dissidents and those who had cooperated with the League of Nations inquiry.

The Tubman years, from 1943 until 1971, ushered in a period of greater cooperative relations between the Americo-Liberians and the interior groups. Tubman's "Open-Door" or "Unification" policy altered the style and substance of settler-"tribal" interaction. President Tubman's more equitable treatment of the hinterland peoples reflected not only his more progressive views, but also, and perhaps more importantly, certain socioeconomic forces which facilitated such policies. Principal among these were the economic development launched by the Firestone Company in the 1920s and, subsequently, by the iron ore companies; the impact of the contacts between Americans and Liberians during the war; the sense of guilt among certain settlers as a result of more extensive involvement with the external world through education overseas and the penetration of the mass media; and finally, the impact of the nationalist movements in the rest of Sub-Saharan Africa.

Tubman expanded education in the hinterland, until then a preserve of the missionaries, restricted the illegal acquisition of land by the settler community, built roads into the interior, and extended the suffrage by lowering the property qualifications and granting women the right to vote.

Despite these innovations, fundamental differences persisted between the settlers and the people of the interior. President Tolbert came to power in 1971 pledging to fight corruption and to narrow further the gap between the Americo-Liberians and the indigenous people. He launched a number of campaigns to achieve these objectives, such as those called "Mat to Mattress," "War on Ignorance," and "Total Involvement." However, the declining demand for iron ore in recent years had an adverse impact on Liberia's economy and made it more difficult to finance a new policy of inclusion. Unwilling to renounce his own business dealings, Tolbert failed to reduce corruption significantly. The narrowing of differences was not tantamount to equality.

The relatively peaceful, if unsatisfactory, coexistence between the Americo-Libericans and the majority people was disrupted April 14, 1979, during the Monrovia riots protesting the proposed government increase in the price of rice. The Progressive Alliance of Liberia (PAL), a group of young students led by Gabriel Baccus Matthews, led the protest. After the leaders were arrested and subsequently released, Tolbert did permit them to transform PAL into an opposition political party, the Peoples Progressive Party (PPP), in January 1980. Even after Matthews called for the resignation of his government and for a general strike at a rally on March 7, 1980, President Tolbert refused to ban the new party.

On April 12, 1980, nearly one year after the rice riots, Tolbert was dead, Master Sergeant Samuel Doe had toppled the government, and the army and the oppressed majority had turned on both the Americo-Liberians and the Congoes.

However, the coup did not remove all dependency upon the Americo-Liberians. After the summary execution of thirteen of the more rapacious officials of the government, Master Sergeant Doe formed a government of reconciliation, which included two representatives of the other opposition group, the Movement for Justice in Africa (MOJA), PPP leaders, the military, and three of Tolbert's ministers.

Calling for a society based upon justice and human dignity shortly after the takeover, Master Sergeant Doe said, "Gone are the days of who do you know and do you know who I am? We now enter a period of what can you do?" What remains to be seen is whether Liberia will be transformed as a result of the April coup or whether the new elite will seek change by mere substitution rather than a total democratization of the society.

NOTE

1. Franz Fanon, "The Pitfalls of National Consciousness," in *The Wretched of the Earth* (London: Hammonsworth, 1969), 122–123.

How Long
Africa's Dependency?
Strategy for Economic
Self-Reliance

Willard R. Johnson

The Proposition

W ITHIN the present international and regional structures and approaches, there is no end in sight for Africa's poverty and its dependency.

The Prerequisites of a Different Future

According to the predictions of a United Nations commissioned study by Nobel laureate Wassily Leontief,[1] even if the modest but unattained targets set in 1975 for the Second Development Decade were to be implemented, there would be no reduction in the income gap between the developed and the "developing" world for the rest of this century. Changes in international aid and trade flows and in the regulations governing access of African and other Third World products to the industrial-country markets and changes in the internal investment levels of such magnitude as to be virtually unimaginable would be required for the gap to begin to close by the year 2000.

Summarizing the findings of the most substantial effort to model the performance of the current global economy, Professor Leontief writes in the *Scientific American* that to achieve the massive transfers necessary to begin to reduce the income gap, one would have to assume that the poorest countries would be permitted to borrow, on very concessional terms, whatever they needed to carry out an appropriate development and import progam. He writes, "the developed regions would be required to work overtime in order to be able to provide the huge amounts of economic aid that would be required under this scenario." Doing so, however, would produce somewhat higher levels of gross national product (GNP) for the developed world and the transfers would result in only a slight reduction of about 3 percent of their GNP. Even so, he concludes that "the practical possibility of carrying out such an optimistic program must be seriously questioned."[2] Some might regard as even less likely the alternative, presumably more practical, approach suggested by the study—the reduction of arms expenditures worldwide by a third from their projected growth rates (resulting in steady 1970s levels in relation to GNP) and transfering much of the savings into development assistance. Under such a scenario, one could reduce the gap between the developed and developing world, if only marginally.

The conditions required to produce growth in the developing world as a whole, growth sufficient to begin to reduce the gap between it and the developed world by the end of the century, suggest substantial changes in both the international and the internal structural relations in the African countries. For non-oil-exporting countries in Africa, an overall growth rate of around 6 percent would be needed, resulting in a two-and-a-half-fold increase in per capita income by the year 2000 (from what it was in 1970) for this region. However, that would bring the level only to about $400 (in 1970 dollars). Achieving even that modest gain (assuming the benefits of rising agricultural and mineral prices, which should lead to larger shares of world markets for these products and boost foreign exchange earnings, which would in turn facilitate needed development-related imports) would require impressive changes in internal investment levels. The share of the final product going to personal consumption would have to fall from the previous level of 70 percent to about 60 percent, and population increase would have to be lowered to about 2 percent.

And, substantial changes would still be required in internal-oriented production. Agriculture and extraction could grow less than the average overall rate of growth in the African economies, but their growth would have to be substantial, nonetheless. It would have to increase at 4 percent per year to provide the three-fold increases needed by 2000. And, heavy industry would have to lead the industrial sector with growth rates of about 7 to 8.5 percent.

Annual aid and investment flows would have to rise quite substantially, especially from North America, Japan, and the centrally planned economies, for significant growth to occur in the developing world generally. (This would be even more necessary for much improvement to occur in Africa.) The general level of U.S. aid would have had to go up to 1 percent of its own GNP by 1980. (U.S. aid did not even begin to approach this target. In fact, generally, levels of aid have fallen during the 1980s.) It would have to go up to 2 percent of GNP by the year 2000. Non-oil Africa would need to have received $3 billion by 1980, $5 billion by 1990, and $47 billion by 2000 (in 1970 dollars) and have levels of average return to foreign investment reduced by two percentage points. As we will see, these were quite impossible targets, judging by the general pattern of performances during the early 1980s.

The Promise of Change

Fundamental change in the international order clearly has been required for quite some time. This need was recognized in both the industrialized and underdeveloped world, although more in the rhetoric than the reality for the former. The call in 1974 for a new international economic order reflected the felt needs of the poor countries. With the rise of OPEC (Organization of Petroleum Exporting Countries) power, it appeared that such changes might be pressed effectively into being.

There was a perceptible change in attitude and stance of the OECD (Organization of Economic Cooperation and Development) countries, provoked by confrontation, but not the old-style confrontation in the tradition of "the brave white hunter" stalking some unsuspecting and isolated prey, a hunter threatened less by the spring of that prey than by the recoil of his own rifle. Now we had a new day—the "cats" had united and "turned the game around." The hunted now stalked the hunters in "packs," to hear tell of it in the alarmed speeches of the likes of Henry Kissinger. Increasingly, the United Nations itself was considered to be merely a pack of the Third World countries. Then there was Yaounde I and Yaounde II, Lima, and the Andean Group, UNCTAD (United Nations Conference on Trade and Development), then the Lome I and Lome II groups. Finally came OPEC and, even more alarming, OAPEC (Organization of Arab Petroleum Exporting Countries). Would the wonders of Allah never cease?

Kissinger's speech (delivered by his truculent UN Ambassador, Daniel Patrick Moynihan) to the Seventh Special Session of the UN General Assembly was an indication of the new situation. He stated that "economic progress has become a central and urgent concern." Where had he been for the preceding two decades? "The economic assistance programs of the 1950s and the 1960s are no longer adequate," he stated. Surely, the Third World had never known them to be adequate.

The Secretary did not limit himself to mere platitudes—he presented concrete goals in five areas: to gain economic security for the underdeveloped countries; to accelerate their growth; to expand opportunities for them to trade; to increase their markets, especially for commodities, such as food; and to address the special needs of the very poorest countries.

He proposed quite a few new institutional and programmatic arrangements: a new Development Security Facility at the International Monetary Fund (IMF); a new International Industrialization Institute; and an International Investment Trust. He also sponsored a new International Energy Institute; a program of generalized tariff preferences for the developing countries; an international system of nationally held grain reserves; the liberalization of IMF support for buffer stocks; and the creation of a consumer-producer forum for every key commodity. He announced that, pending approval by Congress, the United States would sign the tin agreement and would negotiate one for cocoa and sugar. (Later, we did sign a coffee agreement.) He pledged the creation of a revolving fund for natural resources and an IMF Trust Fund for emergency relief. He said the United States would seek to join the African Development Fund and would expand support to the Inter-American Development Bank, the Asian Development Bank, the International Development Agency (IDA), and the IMF-IBRD (International Bank for Reconstruction and Development) Development Committee. There would be expansion of the new International Fund for Agricultural Development (IFAD) and support at the Geneva negotiations on trade for structural improvement in the trading conditions confronting development countries. My! My! Would the wonders of Henry never cease?

It was the most far-reaching and forthcoming promise of change the United States had offered to the Third World, before or since. Still, it was not what the Third World countries themselves had demanded in advancing their call for a new international economic order. More importantly, not all of the programs have been implemented. Once it became apparent that OPEC power was not necessarily enduring, the old patterns reemerged with even greater vigor, especially in the United States, where the Reagan administration began to treat the Third World countries much the way it treated the historically victimized minority ethnic groups and other vulnerable elements of American society.

The Failure to Deliver Change

We will note the more important general outcomes since Kissinger's speech to the Special Session of the UN General Assembly.

The Development Security Facility

Kissinger's proposals were in two parts: the expansion and modification of the IMF's compensatory finance facility and the creation of a trust fund to provide financing for development projects.

First, the finance facility. The IMF Compensatory Finance Facility (CFF) terms were made more lenient. The U.S. delegation returned a week after the Kissinger speech was delivered to present detailed proposals providing for a modification of the 1966 Compensatory Finance Facility with respect to the computation of import-earning shortfall, easing access to the facility, expanding the size of permissible drawings, and modifying the timeframe for full use of the financing. The proposals also called for the creation of linkages with the proposed, but not then created, Trust Fund.

The Special Session did mention in its final resolution a call for stabilization of earnings of developing countries and for the creation of a development security facility and other specific measures for the benefit of the developing countries most in need.

Subsequently, the IMF modified the conditions of operating the Compensatory Finance Facility by increasing the size of drawings but did not limit these new benefits to the developing countries. Thus, the limit was increased by only 75 percent instead of 100 percent. Up to 50 percent of the allocation could be drawn in a twelve-month period. The compensable shortfall was made more liberal than had been proposed by the United States and would permit larger drawings in periods of inflation.[3]

Second, the Trust Fund. On May 6, 1976, the IMF announced that the Trust Fund had been established and that the first gold auction would be in Washington, D.C., on June 2, 1976. Auctions for the sale of one sixth of the Fund's gold (25 million ounces) were scheduled over a four-year period. Profits from sales resulting from the difference between the then special drawing rights (SDR) of 35 per ounce (approximately $41) and the auction price, would go to the Trust Fund.

Sixty-one countries with 1973 per capita incomes of SDR 300 or less were eligible for Trust Fund loans on concessional terms to carry out balance-of-payments adjustment programs. By June 1977, twenty-four loans totalling SDR 152.9 million were made to twenty-four countries. Further loans were scheduled in six-month intervals. By the end of 1980, some fifty-three countries had received over $3.4 billion. The Trust Fund arrangements did not go as far as Kissinger's proposals in permitting loans to be converted into grants. But low interest rates and long repayment periods may make it even more attractive than the Kissinger proposal.[4]

International Industrialization Institute

As of this writing, the institute has not been created. Kissinger's proposal seemed to be an about-face from the position the United States took in Lima at the Second General Conference of the UN Industrial Development Organization (UNIDO), March 12–26, 1975, in which it was the sole vote against the Declaration and Plan of Action on Industrial Development.

The Seventh Special Session endorsed the recommendation to convert the organization into a specialized agency and established an intergovernmental committee of the whole to meet in Vienna (headquarters of UNIDO) to draw up a constitution for UNIDO as a specialized agency.

A subsequent barrier to agreement was that OPEC would not agree to fund shortfalls resulting from the decision of industrial nations not to join.

International Investment Trust

We have no information on the outcome of the International Investment Trust. Perhaps this was treated as the same as the Trust Fund already discussed.

International Energy Institute

As of 1982, this had not yet been established with regard to less developed countries (LDCs). The 1982 *World Bank Annual Report* lamented that "an energy affiliate, a proposal endorsed by the Development Committee in Fiscal Year 1981, remained the most attractive method of raising additional funding for energy investment in developing countries."[5] However, the United States did take further steps in Fiscal Year 1979 to help LDCs develop their own energy resources.

The United States supported expansion of the World Bank's lending program to cover petroleum exploration, as well as production projects, and it was envisioned that IBRD lending for oil and gas projects would increase to about $1.5 billion by 1983.

Other U.S. bilateral efforts included: (1) the Agency for International Development, which assisted LDCs in developing renewable energy technologies; and (2) the Overseas Private Investment Company, which provided insurance coverage for two new energy projects in Egypt and Ghana in Fiscal Year 1979.[6]

General System of Tariff Preferences

Special Session negotiators from the Group of 77, the United States, Japan, Sweden, Australia, Canada, and New Zealand agreed on September 16, 1975, that the General System of Preferences (GSP) was to be continued beyond the original ten years, on improved terms with wider coverage, and that the Multilateral Trade Negotiations (MTN) were to take effective steps to reduce and remove nontariff barriers. Maximum restraint was to be exercised in relation to imposition of countervailing duties on LDC exports.

During the first half of calendar year 1979, total duty-free imports into the United States from developing countries under the GSP amounted to $2.9 billion, as against $2.3 billion in calendar year 1978.

The United States completed its annual review of generalized system of preferences operations in February 1979. Twenty-one new products, with combined trade value of approximately $100 million from beneficiary developing countries, were added to the list (three times the value of additions during 1978), and four products, accounting for $122 million in 1978 duty-free imports, were removed from GSP eligibility.[7]

Grain Reserves

Discussion and examination continued during 1976 on the U.S. proposal for an international system of nationally held grain reserves. These discussions took place within the framework of the International Wheat Council, to consider components of a possible new International Wheat Agreement with provisions for grain reserves. The 1977 *International Economic Report of the President* stated that:

> Although participating governments were able to agree that the reserves should be nationally held and controlled, substantial differences of opinion emerged as to the objectives of the reserves, their size, and the rights and obligations associated with an international grain reserve system. A number of technical questions also arose as to the feasibility of such an arrangement.
>
> In addition, it has become clear since the WFC [World Food Council] that interest in establishing an international grain reserve system to provide world food security has diminished somewhat. This could be due to a variety of factors, especially increased world grain production and rising stocks. Nevertheless, discussions are expected to continue in 1977.[8]

The report questioned the need for a grain reserve over the long haul.

IMF Support for Buffer Stocks

A major breakthrough occurred in the Common Fund negotiations in 1979, with general international agreements that the Fund should facilitate financing of commodity stabilization through buffer stocking "and other measures." An interim committee began work on issues relating to this fund, with the objective of completing negotiations on a detailed text of agreement during the first half of 1980. The articles were agreed upon in June 1980, specifying $400 million in capital. This fund is designed to facilitate the financing of buffer stock activities by pooling International Commodity Agreement (ICA) financial resources.[9]

Commodities Agreements: Coffee, Cocoa, Tin, and Sugar

Commodities agreements did show some advance. In 1976, the United States joined the Tin Council, and intended to remain in the International Coffee Agreement three more years. In 1979, at the fifth session of UNCTAD discussing the reaffirmation and reorientation of the Integrated Program for Commodities (IPC), the United States participated in several international negotiations aimed at reaching agreement on stabilization measures for a number of commodities.

The United States Congress ratified the International Sugar Agreement (negotiated in 1978); completed negotiations for an International Rubber Agreement in 1979, which is to include a 550,000 metric ton buffer stock and a flexible price range; and participated in renegotiation of the expiring cocoa agreement, also in 1979, but these talks were stalled by disagreements over the level of prices at which purchases by the buffer stock would be triggered.[10] The new agreement had failed to win U.S. approval by 1981.

Revolving Fund for Natural Resources

We have no information regarding the revolving fund for natural resources. Perhaps this was treated as part of the buffer stock program previously discussed.

African Development Fund (ADF)

The United States joined ADF in November 1976 with an initial contribution of $15 million, followed by $10 million in 1977, and $25 million in 1978. Total resources pledged to ADF as of September 30, 1979, by all members amounted to $1.147 million. During Fiscal year 1979, ADF loans totaled $207.6 million, distributed among 22 African countries. This was an increase of $52.4 million (34 percent) above the 1978 lending level of $155.2 million. Agricultural projects absorb the greatest share of the loan resources. This pattern is expected to continue.

At the Sixth Annual Meeting of ADF (May 1979), the U.S. representative emphasized the "deep commitment" of the United States to
assist African countries in solving difficult economic problems. The
representative supported establishment of new loan guidelines by
ADF which place greater emphasis on reaching the poor in recipient
countries and on increasing the productivity of small farmers.[11]

Inter-American Development Bank (IDB)

The fifth replenishment period is 1979–1982. The Inter-American
Development Bank completed negotiations on a fifth replenishment
of resources to finance the bank's 1979–1982 lending program. Agreed
subscriptions are $7,969 million in capital resources (exclusive of
unassigned shares), of which 7.5 percent, or $598 million, was to be
paid in.

The United States' contribution to this $7,969 million replenishment
is $2,749 million (34.5 percent of the total), of which $2,543 million
was callable capital and $206 million paid-in capital. In the 1979–82
Replenishment Agreement for the Inter-American Development Bank,
substantial progress was made toward meeting U.S. goals in terms
of increasing IDB lending to the poor, achieving more equitable burden
sharing among member countries, and reducing U.S. budget outlays.
Members of the bank agreed to contribute $1,750 million to the IDB
Fund for Special Operations (FSO) over the 1979–1982 period, of which
the United States was to contribute $700 million (40 percent of the
total).[12] From 1979 to 1982, the U.S. share of both IDB capital and
Funds for Special Operations resources will decline, while nonregional
members will assume, as a group, a share two-and-one-half times
their current share.

Increased burden sharing has enabled the United States to reduce
the level of its annual contribution to FSO from $200 million of the
last previous replenishment to $175 million during the 1979–1982 fifth
replenishment period. Agreement also provides for a 25 percent reduction in percentage of capital to be paid in. These measures, combined,
will permit the United States to reduce its outlays for FSO and capital
by $13 million annually during the fifth replenishment period.

Asian Development Bank (ADB) and the African Development Fund (ADF)

In 1979, the membership was 43 countries (29 regional and 14 nonregional). ADB lending in Fiscal Year 1978 was $996 million; in Fiscal
Year 1979, it was $985 million. Of Fiscal Year 1979 loans, a total of

$583 million was funded with ADB ordinary capital and $402 million with the concessional resources of the bank. The cumulative total ADB lending as of September 30, 1979 (for the period from 1966 to 1979) amounted to $5,730 million, of which $4,014 million was ordinary capital funding and $1,716 million concessional funding. During Fiscal Year 1979, the United States subscribed to $194.5 million of ordinary capital shares, raising total U.S. subscriptions to ADB capital to $1,055 million (out of total subscribed capital of $8,842), giving the United States a 10 percent voting share. The United States also contributed $70 million to the resources of the African Development Fund, raising the total U.S. contributions to ADF to $270 million (out of total contributions of $2,093 million from all sources).

During 1978, negotiations were completed for the second replenishment of the AD Fund to finance the ADF 1979–1982 lending program. The second replenishment became effective in 1979, when instruments of contribution representing funds in excess of $1 billion were received from a number of donor countries. The U.S. contribution, subject to congressional authorization and appropriation, will be $445 million over a four-year period, or about $111 million annually from 1980 to 1983. This contribution represents 20.7 percent of the $2.15 billion replenishment, including voluntary contributions.

IDA

The IDA fifth replenishment (1977 through June 1980) is $7,732 million, designed to cover lending need through June 1980. The U.S. contribution to the fifth replenishment equals $2,400 million, to be made available in equal installments over a three-year period, subject to congressional appropriations. First and second installments were appropriated by Fiscal Years 1978 and 1979 legislation. Legislation has been submitted for final installment of the fourth replenishment and for the fifth replenishment. During Fiscal Year 1979, IDA extended new credits in the amount of $2,289 million to help support 108 development projects. Cumulative credits held by IDA as of September 30, 1979, amounted to $17,081 million.

In 1979 the Development Committee met to discuss the status of problems confronting developing countries. During the discussion, the United States indicated its belief that no generalized financial crisis was then facing the developing countries and that available resources in existing institutions were adequate to finance balance-of-payment needs.

The Development Committee then made several recommendations to the IMF and IBRD Boards of Executive Directors. (1) For the Fund, the recommendation was made to extend the repurchasing period in the Extended Fund Facility (EFF) from 8 to 120 years and to lower the Supplementary Financing Facility (SFF) interest costs. (2) For IBRD, the committee supported the bank's stated intention to consider increasing program lending substantially and called on the board to explore criteria covering the extension of program loans in cases where balance-of-payments problems might be developing in the future.

In 1980, legislation to authorize U.S. participation in the sixth re-plenishment of the IDA was submitted but not passed by the time of the Reagan administration, which threatened to cut back on the U.S. commitment. Due to subsequently lower levels of U.S. support, the World Bank had to slash by 40 percent its level of subsidized loans to developing countries. The total IDA loan level fell to $2.6 billion from an anticipated level of $4.1 billion. To counteract these reductions, the World Bank made available an additional $800 million in loan funds but had to charge higher rates than normal for this support. Middle-income countries were encouraged to borrow on com-merical rates.[13]

Trading Conditions

A mixed picture also emerges regarding the issues of improving trading conditions for developing countries. Concerning stabilization of export earnings, representatives of the developing countries called for the establishment of a new commodity facility, disagreeing with the view that the CFF liberalization was adequate to meet their needs. The United States took the position that the recent liberalization of the CFF was sufficient to smooth over periods of shortfalls in export earnings.[14]

With regard to the proposed International Fund for Agricultural Development, the UN conference, June 10–13, 1976, in Rome "adopted and initialled an agreement establishing the International Fund for Agricultural Development (IFAD) which will be opened for formal signature AS SOON AS THE TARGET OF $1,000 MILLION in convert-ible currencies is reached. Thus, the conference cleared the way for the setting up of a new United Nations specialized agency–IFAD."[15]

The IFAD would have to target the problem of the slow growth rate of food production in many developing countries: "If the slow growth trends of the first half of the 1970s continue unchanged, developing countries could have an annual cereal deficit of 100 million tons a year by 1985."[16]

Pledges to the IFAD came slowly. By mid-1976 they amounted to

$940 million, of which OPEC's Special Fund accounted for $400 million, Industrialized Nations' contributions for $530 million, and IFAD for $10 million (in convertible and nonconvertible currencies). The original plans of the Preparatory Commission were to call a January 1977 meeting if the Fund's targets were not reached within six months.

The proposal to set up the Fund had been one of the most important resolutions adopted by the World Food Conference held in Rome in 1974. At the Seventh Special Session in 1975, the General Assembly emphasized the urgency of the need for early creation of the fund and, at its thirtieth regular session, the General Assembly decided to convene the UN Conference on the Establishment of the Fund, to adopt and open for signature the agreement for its creation.[17]

Regarding the International Fund for Agricultural Development, Kissinger said the United States would support IFAD with a $200-million contribution if $800 million was forthcoming from OECD and OPEC countries. Other major issues at the Rome conference were resolving the financing, management, and operations of IFAD and initiating an agreement by ninety-one countries to establish the Fund.[18]

The agreement established the Fund with initial capital of $1 billion, to be used for projects and programs to increase food supply in developing countries.

The IFAD itself would have the following characteristics: (1) be a specialized agency relying heavily on the international financial institutions for assistance to achieve its goals; (2) be capitalized at $1 billion initially; (3) have three categories of members: (a) developed contributors, (b) OPEC contributors, and (c) developing country recipients; and (4) like IDA, give grants and concessional loans.

During 1979, the IFAD Executive Board approved twenty-three projects amounting to approximately $382 million equivalent. All of these were to be cofinanced with other multilateral development agencies. IFAD plans to increase the number of projects it initiates during 1980. Replenishment of IFAD resources could be needed by mid-1981.[19] The 1982 World Bank Report indicates that it participated in fifty-four projects with the IFAD, which it said was slightly more than half of the total number of projects supported by that institution.

Geneva Negotiations: 1974–1979

On April 12, 1979, the negotiations resulted in six major codes of trade conduct, balanced concessions in tariffs, increased market access, new rules in agricultural trade, modernization of the international trading system, and sectoral agreements on trade in steel and aircraft. In the United States, policy coordination was strengthened in the Office of the U.S. Trade Representative (formerly STR), and the Commerce Department was given a larger operational role in export promotion activities and the administration of statutes covering unfair trade practices.

The Export-Import Bank lending authority was also increased substantially. Loans authorized by the bank to overseas buyers of U.S. equipment and services increased by 20 percent, from $2.9 billion in Fiscal Year 1978 to $3.7 billion in Fiscal Year 1979. Gross authorization by the bank rose 30 percent, from $7.4 to $9.6 billion, over the same period.[20]

Reagan's Caribbean Basin Initiative did provide for beneficial changes in the access to U.S. markets for Caribbean exports and gave incentives for U.S. investment in the area.

The Aid Picture for Africa

Secretary Kissinger certainly was right in describing the programs of the 1950s and the 1960s as inadequate. We see from his proposals that his concerns expressed in the Seventh Special Session of the General Assembly did inaugurate quite a number of important innovations. Yet, these innovations remained insufficient. The deficiency of these changes should be judged against the requirements for growth and development, however, and not merely against what had existed before and not in relation to the requirements of stemming the impetus in the poor regions to engage in confrontation diplomacy.

Even in the 1970s, during a period of confrontation, the assistance remained inadequate. In 1974, Kissinger predicted that by 1980 the "developing world" (what was and still is a euphemism) would require $40 billion a year in capital assistance (not food, balance of payments, or recurrent budget assistance). Estimating from what is available through the early 1980s, it is safe to say that total economic assistance flows, bilateral and multilateral for all purposes, amounted to less than three-fourths that amount.[21]

The flows of U.S. economic assistance have never been great, either in absolute terms or in relation to U.S. national income. For the period from 1962 through 1975, for example, total U.S. net flow of resources (including investment) to less developed countries amounted to only about $98 billion. Less than half of this, or about $47 billion, was in the form of official development assistance, and only $30 billion of that was in the form of grants ($27 billion in bilateral and $3 billion in multilateral grants). The rest was in the form of loans and debt relief. Judging by other U.S. sources that give somewhat higher figures from this same period, total U.S. economic assistance, net of loan repayments, averaged only about $6.5 to $7.0 billion per year during the Carter Presidency.[22] Much of the U.S. aid has always been in the form of emergency and famine food relief ($23 billion of the $82 billion total between 1962 and 1979, for example.)

By 1980, official development assistance from all the OECD countries was little higher as a proportion of their GNP than it had been in 1975 and only about half of the .70 percent of GNP that most of them had accepted as a reasonable target figure. Their collective performance was heavily influenced by the disappointing record of the largest donor, the United States. In 1980, aid of the OECD countries was only .43 percent of their combined GNP, excluding the United States, which provided only .27 percent of GNP. Sweden, Norway, Denmark, and The Netherlands all exceed the .70 percent target level.[23]

Net capital receipts of the low-income oil importers did not increase at all after 1975 in real terms. Real Official Development Assistance (ODA) receipts in 1979 and 1980 were, in fact, lower than the 1975 level. There was no increase in the flow of commercial loans, so that the poor countries received no increase in support to help ease the burdens of the 1979–1980 trade losses associated with the second oil crisis and other industrial product inflation.[24] Thus, it is clear that the predicted capital needs are far from being met.

Africa's share of the official U.S. economic assistance has always been small, including figures for Egypt and the North African countries that have received the lion's share of Africa's assistance, usually in consideration of military alliance requirements, even prior to the Camp David Accords. The figure for the continent during the years from 1962 to 1979 totaled only about $6 billion (net of loan repayments), of which more than a third was in the form of food. The portion available for capital purchases would amount to only about $3.8 billion for the seventeen-year period or less than what African now needs *yearly* for capital formation assistance.

U.S. officials have always argued that the bulk of the needed external capital inputs in the developing world would be available only through private investment flows, which would have the (presumed) added advantage of providing scarce management know-how and marketing and technology connections. Private investment will hardly meet the need if past trends continue, however. The 1975 United Nations study of multinational corporations in world development showed that the eighteen market-oriented, developed countries made a net investment of only about $8 billion outside that group during the six years from 1965 through 1970. Unfortunately for the "developing" areas, the payments of interest, dividends, and earnings on the previous investment drained them of a net $19 billion, after taking the new investment into account, a loss financed largely by the "economic assistance" programs that were meant to stimulate new development.

Trade relations, unquestionably the most important source of foreign exchange receipts for the developing countries, are also still insufficiently positive to permit the underdeveloped countries to reverse their standing in the world economy. One part of the problem is that the exports of the underdeveloped countries have tended to suffer deteriorating prices in relation to the prices of the industrial product imports these countries require for their economic progress. The United Nations Conference on Trade and Development has estimated[25] that the net barter terms of trade of the underdeveloped countries declined by 12 percent between 1954 and 1970, causing a loss to them of $10 billion for the period 1960–1972. Despite some benefits to commodity prices just prior to the first "oil crisis," the strength of relative prices for the products of the underdeveloped world have continued to show weakness. The World Bank study entitled *Accelerated Development in Sub-Saharan Africa* indicates that net barter terms of trade for this region were the same in 1979 as in 1975, with some gains by oil exporters counterbalancing deterioration of the low-income semiarid countries.

Conclusion

It is clear that as the decade of the 1970s drew to a close, international capital flows, market relationships, and internal as well as world economic structures had not yet begun to show the changes necessary for Africa, along with much of the rest of the impoverished world, to improve its relative economic standing or meet the needs and basic desires of its people. Hope for such changes was sparked by the dramatic power and income shifts that the OPEC countries were able to achieve and by the subsequent changes in rhetoric and policy of the United States and some other industrial countries. Although much of the program suggested at the Seventh Special Session of the UN was implemented, this occurred at too low a level of funding and within too restricted a scope to reverse the trends. The follow-up efforts were not insubstantial, just insufficient. This all suggests that tampering with the international relationships will not be enough. Fundamental changes must occur.

It is questionable whether Africa could sufficiently buffer its economies from the effects of the global system by withdrawal from it. It is even more difficult to imagine the will to withdraw being exercised by the leadership that currently rules most of the continent. The revolutionary forces are still weak in almost all of Africa. Thus, we are not likely to see a leadership emerging that will be willing and able to accept a near total break with consumer luxuries for the period required to reorient African production into goods that meet the basic needs and wants of its own people first, that provide a basis for importing more advanced technology while improving domestic sources of technical innovation, training, and propagation, and that put emphasis on the use of local resources.

What does all this mean for those interested in promoting genuine economic development in Africa, whether they be part of American, Afro-American, or African society? One thing is clear. It is wishful thinking to expect recent approaches and arrangements to make any substantial difference in our lifetimes.[26]

The past economic relationships between the developed and the underdeveloped and dependent world have been ones of exploitation of the most gross sort. The fact that economic planning and policy making and economic performance in the African countries have been grossly deficient does not make this any the less true or relevant. The fact that justified charges of external exploitation are made by high-living officials of controlled societies that derive as much of their power base from these very international relationships as from any internally rooted legitimacy also should not blind our eyes to the internal policy changes that will be needed for development to begin to occur.

On both sides of the ocean, we must begin to build an enlightened and powerful, daring constituency of political support for balanced, equitable, and corrective relationships and policies. This is likely to require a place for the people's voice in both domestic and international policy making. In the end, everyone may be forced to choose sides between the hunters and the hunted. There will be less and less neutral ground.

For those of us in America, this is not a question of choosing America or choosing its enemies. Americans, even Afro-Americans, are often their own enemy. Rather, it is basically a question of what kind of America we wish it to be. For those in Africa it seems the question is similar: What kind of Africa is it that we wish to bring into being?

NOTES

I wish to thank Ms. Carol Conaway and Ms. Cathy Boone, doctoral candidates in the M. I. T. Political Science Department, for the splendid research assistance they rendered in tracking the implementation of the proposals of the Seventh Special Session. I also gratefully acknowledge the financial support from the Ford Foundation for this research assistance and other research inputs into this paper.

1. Wassily Leontief, *inter alia, The Future of the World Economy: A United Nations Study* (New York: Oxford University Press, 1977).
2. *Scientific American* (September, 1980).
3. *UN Chronicle* 1979; and National Advisory Commission on International Monetary and Fiscal Policy, *Annual Report to the U.S. President,* Fiscal Year 1979 (hereafter, NAC-ARP).
4. *UN Chronicle* 1979; and NAC-ARP FY79.
5. World Bank, *World Development Report 1982,* 38.
6. NAC-ARP, FY79.
7. NAC-ARP, FY79.
8. U.S. Government Printing Office, *International Economic Report of the President,* 1977, 61.
9. NAC-ARP, FY79.
10. NAC-ARP, FY79.
11. NAC-ARP, FY79.
12. NAC-ARP, FY79.
13. *Facts on File,* No. 122, G1-A2.
14. NAC-ARP, FY79.
15. *U.N. Chronicle,* vol. 12, no. 7, 38.
16. *Ibid.*
17. *Ibid.*
18. IFAD, Draft Cooperation Agreement, IBRD, Section M77-538, 29 June 1977.
19. *UN Chronicle* 1979; and NAC-ARP, FY79.
20. NAC-ARP FY79.
21. See the *International Economic Report of the President,* 1977. I assume multilateral levels to be roughly half the total. In 1979 this was $14 billion.
22. See United States Agency for International Development, Office of Planning and Budgeting, *U.S. Overseas Loans and Grants and Assistance from International Organizations,* 1980, 6, 143.
23. World Bank, *World Development Report 1981,* 50.
24. *Ibid.,* 53.
25. See the *Handbook of International Trade and Development Statistics.*
26. For an update into the early 1980s of the issues discussed in this paper, see Willard K. Johnson, "Reform or Revolution," in Anyong Nyong'o, ed., *State and Social Transformation in Africa: Authority and Capacity to Rule* (Trenton, N.J.: Africa World Press, forthcoming 1987).

Response

George Williams

IN reviewing the paper presented by Professor Johnson, there are three important aspects worthy of comment for the discussion.

The first aspect concerns the variance between the promise, specifically the U.S. aid to developing countries, and the actual performance of the donor and, in fact, the impact of such assistance. In his view, we must evaluate the performance against some standard or norm, such as the requirement for growth and development along a given path. In this light, U.S. aid, although substantial, has been inadequate both in absolute terms and in relation to the U.S. national income.

He further questions the form U.S. aid has taken and its contribution to local capital formation. The aid has gone mostly into food relief and security assistance, among other areas. According to this view, the prerequisite for steady economic growth in the developing world in the predictable future would lie in the expansion of world trade and in creating growing markets for Third World manufactured goods. But in looking at this view, we see that the prerequisites here expand further the need for reliance on the very factors from which the paper seems to suggest we should withdraw, that is, reliance on the developed countries. In spite of various trade and economic agreements, we have seen that the products of the developing world have not gained access to industrial markets. In fact, the situation remains such that an export-oriented drive has not produced broad-based economic development. Rather, the basic products on which the developing countries have depended have experienced a drop in their relative attractiveness in the developed countries. In addition, their manufactured goods, on which they had pinned high hopes, have not been accepted in the developed countries because of tariff and nontariff barriers. So we see that expansion of export trade may not necessarily lessen their dependency relationship.

Second, Johnson's paper is critical of the role envisioned for foreign private investment by, say, U.S. foreign assistance officials. He challenges the concept that private investment, not economic assistance, is the only avenue by which capital formation should be accomplished. Further, in his view, foreign capital investment can have a negative effect, particularly in the balance of payments, resulting in a net out-flow of interests, dividends, and repatriated capital generated by the private investment in the developing countries. This argument, while being quite true, I think, has some missing elements, including the role played by private investment, be it ever so limited in the developing context, in actually stimulating local capital formation, however limited that may be.

The final aspect points to the dilemma actually facing the African and Third World policy makers who must harness the political will and where-with-all necessary to move their countries from the present dependency relationship to self-reliance in the face of these undesirable choices between inadequate aid resources and the uncertain benefits of private capital investment.

To analyze, within the context of Professor Johnson's paper, the link between self-reliance and economic development, we may want to exact a definition of *self-reliance*. The concept of *self-reliance* itself has undergone considerable modification and change in the context of the increasingly interdependent world in which we find ourselves. As Africans and Afro-Americans, we are all in favor of self-reliance, but there are serious problems to be confronted on every particular path which self-reliance may take. Professor Johnson defines a possible path which calls for rechanneling production away from luxuries, so that the African nations will begin to develop the ability to undertake a number of important tasks, such as, for example, producing goods to supply the basic requirements and needs for their people, stimulating domestic technology and innovation, developing and infusing manpower skills, and, finally, I may add, making worthy use of local resources.

I would suggest that while self-reliance remains a laudable goal, there can be no consensus of the particular time frame required to achieve it. Given the present state of world economic affairs, where the current-account deficits of the developing countries are, in fact, actually related to their need to finance this sort of economic development, there is consequently a need for you and me to view self-reliance not so much in terms of buffering the Africans from the effects of the present global world system, but rather, in terms of improving the efficiency in the use of available resources.

Professor Johnson also suggested that priority might be accorded more inward-looking policies. For example, using industry, as I mentioned before, not to produce consumer luxuries but rather to supply the basic needs and wants. I would say again that it is questionable whether such a policy would gain substantial political support, as mentioned in the paper because we see that the sacrifice necessary to make this come about incurs a cost which political leaders and policy makers apparently are unwilling to pay at this particular time (when the benefits which would result are too far in the future, perhaps, to permit them to take any credit).

Professor Johnson, I feel, was correct in not identifying the requirements of self-reliance in terms of the changing patterns of investment, trade, production, and consumption. But, I feel, what is lacking is the idea that self-reliance should be placed within the context of optimal use of available resources. This process and the proposal recommended by Professor Johnson—that productive efficiency takes priority over the choice of goods to be produced—are the crucial elements in meeting the problem.

Teaching and Research Resources on Afro-Americans in Africa

Joseph E. Harris

OVER the last decade or so African and Afro-American studies have witnessed an increased emphasis on the historical connection between Africans and their descendants in the Americas. Evidence of that trend may be seen in the growing number of academic conferences and publications focusing on African/Afro-American relations, quite apart from Pan-Africanism as traditionally understood in political terms.

Howard University Press has published *Global Dimensions of the African Diaspora*, a collection of twenty-four papers presented at the First African Diaspora Studies Institute at Howard University in 1979. Essays in that volume assess the concept and methodologies of the African diaspora, analyze networks through case studies, and provide a perceptive description of personal experiences by scholars and practitioners of Pan-Africanism.

What is particularly significant about the volume is that it presents serious pieces by continental African scholars who used oral and written sources to reconstruct African/Afro-American relations in African societies and includes evidence of contact through individuals and organizations that had no conscious political ideologies. That is a reflection of what St. Clair Drake characterizes as pan-Africanism (with a small "p"). Church groups, educational projects, personal visits, various kinds of conferences as well as financial and other kinds of contributions by Afro-Americans were part of that phenomenon. This Liberia seminar falls into that category.

99

Much of the momentum for this recent emphasis on African diaspora studies has come from the several conferences convened by UNESCO and Howard University, among others. In particular, the UNESCO "Meeting of Experts on the Cultures of the Caribbean," which convened at Santo Domingo, Dominican Republic in 1978, addressed a number of important issues and adopted an item of crucial relevance: "the African presence, which was often ignored or minimized, should be unequivocally admitted to whatever definition [of Caribbean culture] formulated by the conference, since it is the axis around which the whole contemporary Caribbean culture was built up." This view epitomized the thrust of the concern for African diaspora studies among blacks in the Caribbean.

The First African Diaspora Studies Institute examined the status of teaching and research in African diaspora studies in Africa and the Americas and explored the possibility of strengthening links between African and American scholars and teachers in the field. Delegates from Africa, Europe, the Caribbean, and the United States discussed conceptual and methodological issues as well as historical and geopolitical scope. Each delegate from Africa presented a report on the number and type of courses taught at his or her university and assessed the possibilities of adding more courses. There was also a discussion of teaching techniques and materials.

That conference ended after having adopted a number of recommendations, including:

the call for a follow-up conference within two to three years;
the study of the possibility that a newsletter or journal be launched in African diaspora studies; and
the appeal for funds to provide resource scholars and library materials to support the development of African diaspora studies at African universities.

In January 1980, the director general of UNESCO, Amadou-Mahtar M'Bow, called on the participants at a conference held in Barbados on "The African Cultural Presence in the Caribbean and in North and South America" to meet the challenge by defining and giving specificity "to the scope, contours and socio-cultural context of the African Diaspora." He also asked the delegates to recommend research projects and other activities for UNESCO's involvement.

The following key proposals were submitted by the delegates at the Barbados conference:

the integration of studies on the African diaspora into school programs of American countries;

the translation and distribution to interested institutions of relevant materials on the African cultural presence in the Americas;

the encouragement of radio stations to broadcast programs relating to the African diaspora and black culture; and

the preparation of a general history of the African peoples in the Americas.

In addition to those recommendations, the following two formulas were proposed for the achievement of the conference's aims:

the creation of a cultural association whose members should come from Africa and the diaspora; and

the establishment of an advisory committee to identify, select, and supervise the publication and translation of basic documents, archival sources, and relevant books and to coordinate the distribution of those materials.

The Howard conference and the UNESCO meetings are relevant to this seminar because they stressed the importance of teaching and research in the area of African diaspora studies. In addition, the Second African Diaspora Studies Institute, which convened over a hundred delegates at the University of Nairobi in 1981, had essentially the same concerns, namely, the assessment of the status of research and teaching in African diaspora studies. Papers were presented on selected topics in the field, syllabi and research checklists from several African countries were examined, and ways of continuing the collective contact were also considered.

A fundamental objective of the conferences at Howard University and the University of Nairobi was to encourage African universities to teach and conduct research in the field. This matter is especially crucial to the development of such studies because Africa is central to the African diaspora concept. Indeed, that concept is viable only is if its sustained in Africa as well as abroad. African scholars and writers must emphasize this African dimension abroad as a critical element in both the reconstruction of the African heritage and contempory international politics. Such realities require a reorientation in the conceptualization of the African heritage in which the Afro-American experience is understood as an extension of African history.

This is a propitious time for African universities to exercise their full impact in this trend. They are now in a position to reorient their programs away from the constraints of the colonial administrations which, among other things, denied and excluded from study any meaningful organic historical relationship between Africans and their descendants abroad. The following examples confirm that a number of African universities are, indeed, part of the recent trend in this area of study.

The Université de Yaoundé has a number of departments in which African descendants abroad receive scholarly treatment; however, American studies, in general, and Afro-American studies, in particular, appear prominently in the programs of the Departments of History and Literature. In the Department of History, for example, there is a coordinated program of discrete units in American studies with an emphasis on the history of Afro-Americans, or as it is called there, "Black Studies." This is an optional program for undergraduates and is popular among the students. In addition, the Department of Literature publishes a journal, *Abbia*, which devotes attention to African descendants abroad.

Teaching and research about the African heritage abroad are conducted at the Université d'Abidjan in the Departments of Modern Languages, History, and English and in the Institute of Negro-African Literature and Aesthetics. The history department considers the subject in courses on the slave trade, slavery and abolition, and Pan-Africanism; the English department includes consideration of the Harlem Renaissance, the civil rights movement, black nationalism, and Afro-American writers in the United States and the Caribbean. The institute concentrates on literature and aesthetics of the black world, and research there has focused on the works of James Baldwin, Booker T. Washington, W. E. B. Du Bois, and others.

The University of Nairobi has a number of departments in which the African diaspora is considered. For nearly ten years, the Department of History has offered a course entitled, "Africa and the Black Diaspora," and the Department of Literature offers courses on Afro-American literature, Caribbean literature, and black aesthetics. Although I did not confirm it, I understand that Kenyatta University also has courses on the African presence abroad.

Because of its size, resources, and long contacts with Afro-Americans, including many students in black American colleges and universities, Nigeria has the most extensive programs on the African diaspora. Courses range over many disciplines: Afro-American and Caribbean literature, Afro-American music, slavery in Africa and the United States, black communities in the New World since emancipation, history of Pan-Africanism, drama of black Americans and the Caribbean, civil rights in the United States, and others. The University of Calabar has the most elaborate selection of courses, not only in Nigeria but in all of Africa.

The University of Nsukka, in addition to offering a variety of courses in the field, established in 1963 the William Leo Hansberry African

Studies Institute, named after the prominent Afro-American historian of Africa at Howard University, 1922–1959. The University of
Ibadan's offerings on Caribbean and United States blacks also pursue
the diaspora perspective by offering a course entitled, "The Freetown
Creoles in West Africa," a dimension of what may be called the "internal diaspora."

One should also note that following the Festival of African Culture
(FESTAC) in 1977, which assembled experts on African and black
culture from around the world, Nigeria established the Center for
Black and African Arts and Culture in Lagos. That center is administered by the Ministry of Information to promote research on black
world communities, facilitate dialogues among black people, and forge
cooperation between Africa and the diaspora.

While the Université de Dakar covers aspects of the black diaspora
in only a few general courses in the Departments of History, Literature, and English, the Foundation de Léopold Sédar Senghor is devoted to the development of studies on black culture throughout the
world and has pursued contacts with scholars and organizations for
that purpose.

The Malawian and Zambian delegates to the Howard conference
have reported that their universities have adopted a course on the
African diaspora. The University of Zambia also approved a course
on United States history. The Nairobi delegate from the University of
Zimbabwe has reported that he introduced a course on "The African
Experience in the Diaspora" and plans to initiate a course on slavery
in the Americas.

These selected examples illustrate a serious African interest in the
black diaspora. While most of the university courses offered are optional and although several of them are not regularly taught, and
even though it appears that several universities on the continent only
consider the subject in nondiaspora courses, many do provide a selection of discrete courses which confirm a commitment to the subject.
Indeed, many African scholars, administrators, writers, and students
have expressed the need for cultivating and sustaining interest and
efforts through meaningful links between African and diaspora universities and other institutions.

Effective teaching requires serious research, which several African
scholars have cited as a major problem due to the limited documentation in Africa. The Howard and Nairobi conferences confirmed that
problem but demonstrated that it has been exaggerated. A number
of the African delegates at the Nairobi conference, for example, had
investigated the holdings in their national archives to determine the
extent of available sources for research. They prepared checklists of

their findings, which were discussed at the conference. Those check-lists identified a number of documents with data on the immigration of Afro-Americans to several African countries from the nineteenth century to the present. Documents also revealed a much greater African awareness of and interest in Marcus Garvey and his Universal Negro Improvement Association than we have thus far read, especially in the French-speaking countries. The influence of Afro-American missionaries, educationists, trade unionists, and students is also revealed in a number of those documents as well as the financial contributions diaspora blacks made to Africans, especially students. The data from those, and other, sources (including oral testimonies) would support individual and collaborative research to locate points of settlement of Afro-Americans in Africa and facilitate the examination of the ways in which those immigrants were received by specific host societies, the processes and results of adjustment, and the degree of impact on African ideas and development.

It is becoming increasingly clear that Afro-Americans in the transfer of administrative and technical ideas and skills helped in the development of a number of African societies. It is also clear that Afro-Americans returned to the Americas influenced by the homeland. Studies designed to explore these issues would greatly enhance our understanding of the African/Afro-American Connection and would become another means of sustaining links between African and black American individuals and institutions.

African interest in this field is accompanied by a recognition that assistance is needed. Most African scholars and teachers have not been trained in the subject and are thus uneasy about assuming a central role in its development, especially if no support system is provided. Several delegates at a number of conferences have suggested the formulation of a program of diaspora studies at universities in the United States with fellowships available for African students. Another suggestion is that summer institutes be conducted in Africa to train faculty already holding academic positions at African universities. And, of course, there is universal recognition that there must be additional materials available in libraries if university programs in the field are to develop properly.

At the final session of the Nairobi conference, the delegates voted to organize the International African Diaspora Studies Association. A committee was elected on a geographical basis to provide continuity for the group, prepare proposals for organizational structure, explore the feasibility of holding another conference, establish a research institute, and publish a newsletter.

The idea of an African diaspora newsletter was first presented at the

Howard conference in 1979 and later at the Barbados meeting in 1980. UNESCO has since awarded a small grant to Howard University to fund a newsletter pilot project, which will appear in English, French, Spanish, and Portuguese. The newsletter will seek to identify works which should be translated and distributed in different parts of the world; publish reports on relevant developments in communities of African descent in different countries; announce itineraries of scholars, writers, performers, and others in the field; and support the development of an international African diaspora studies network of specialists and interested lay persons around the world. To date, letters of support for the newsletter have come from individuals in over thirty-five countries in North, South, and Central America, the Caribbean, Europe, and Africa. The first issue is scheduled to appear in late 1983.

The results of all of these activities constitute a major challenge and a new direction in the study of the African/Afro-American Connection. There is a heightened awareness that African people are an integral and extended part of a world in which momentous economic and intellectual forces continue to shape political, social, and economic structures, thereby causing reorientation of perspectives and realignment of constituencies in Africa, the diaspora, and elsewhere. By both their presence and actions in the midst of a Euro-American-dominated system, men and women of African descent continue to influence and be influenced by decisions made in that system.

As a historical part of that phenomenon, Africans in the diaspora contributed to the development and appreciation of the concept of the nation-state in Africa. At a time when most continental Africans defined their societies primarily along ethnic and familial lines and Europeans defined them as "barbarous tribes," several Afro-Americans promoted the idea of the nation-state in Africa, both as an end and as a means of challenging derogatory stereotypes about the ability of African people to govern, survive, and progress.

It was within that context that Africans abroad supported the liberation of Haiti, the repatriation experiments of Sierra Leone and Liberia, the establishment of the Mandates and, later, Trusteeship systems, the expulsion of the Italians from Ethiopia in the 1930s, and the continental freedom movements of the twentieth century. In addition, diaspora Africans became pioneer teachers, civil servants, journalists, physicians, and missionaries throughout much of Africa. Diaspora Africans have shared their limited resources to educate continental Africans in the United States, and their ideas have increasingly inspired freedom struggles throughout the black world.

It is especially significant that those ideas and actions as applied to Africa by blacks during the slave trade and colonial eras were innovative and provided a basis for an evolving international consciousness of black identity in the United States, the Caribbean, and Africa. Noteworthy as that was, however, the sense of national and Pan-African development, which Afro-Americans promoted, incorporated African and Western values and posed dilemmas that we continue to face. We must, therefore, be careful not to exaggerate the role of diaspora Africans, and we certainly must evaluate any positive and negative impacts they had. Additionally, we need to examine data in the diaspora, not only to enhance our understanding of Afro-Americans in Africa but also to evaluate the impact of the continental African in the diaspora. While that is not the agenda for this particular conference, we should remain aware of that dimension of our relationship.

In sum, serious analytical attention should be devoted to the teaching and research of the historical and contemporary linkages between Africa and the diaspora. This conference on the African/Afro-American Connection is thus a significant contribution to that objective.

Response

Eustace Palmer

IN reading Professor Harris's paper, I was struck by its conciseness. It seems a straightforward, very concise, and very lucid account of the kinds of activities that go on in American universities and also in African universities insofar as teaching and research into African studies is concerned. My response is going to be more brief than that of other discussants, partly because I find myself substantially in agreement with most of what Professor Harris has said. I will use a slightly different emphasis, however. For instance, when he talks about the topics of research, it seems to me he emphasized what he calls *linkages*; he emphasized the contribution that Afro-Americans have made to African society and that Africans have made to Afro-American society. This, of course, is splendid, and a lot of that is going on. I would like to concentrate, however, on what I think Africans should do. I think, perhaps they ought to be studying the culture of Afro-American society, the nature of the Afro-American personality, and perhaps the pressures to which Afro-Americans are subjected, even though Africans may also consider themselves within the linkages. For instance, I think that an African scholar may wish to investigate the literature of the Afro-American. This may or may not have anything to do with linkage, but I think it will still be important. Or an African may want simply to investigate the elements of Afro-American music. This is the kind of thing on which I would like to concentrate.

I will respond to Professor Harris's paper by dealing with the subject under four headings relevant to teaching and research, examining in some detail the constraints, I think, in which African universities have to operate. Professor Harris has, of course, mentioned some of these in passing, but I would like to develop them further. The four headings I will use are (1) restructuring the curriculum—both the school curriculum and the university curriculum—which he mentioned in his paper, in order to introduce Afro-American studies to our own students; (2) resource materials—for teaching, research, and staff training—a matter he gives some prominence in his paper; (3) provision of funds—extremely important to us—a topic he touched on but which I would like to elaborate on; and (4) the kinds of research I think we ought to be engaged in.

Restructuring the Curriculum

Professor Harris mentioned in his paper that we Africans are now in a position to reorganize our curricula and to move away from the colonial educational pattern. This, of course, is absolutely true, for this is going on at the moment in our curriculum exercise. In this reorganized curriculum, Afro-American studies or diaspora studies are also featured. We quite often talk about the ignorance of Afro-Americans about African society. But I think at times we ought to talk about the ignorance of Africans, especially African children, African youngsters, about Afro-American society. It seems to me that the thing works both ways; and if Dr. Harris suggests that we must introduce diaspora studies or information about Africans to Afro-American students in their schools, it can also be said, with some justification, that we ought to introduce knowledge and information about Afro-Americans to our students, both in the schools and in the universities. He has given an impressive list of the kinds of activities that are going on at universities in Africa—Nsukka, Calabar, Yaoundé, and so on. My impression, in spite of the list he has given, is that this effort is still rather piecemeal, that Afro-American studies are not taught per se, but perhaps, I think, he admits somewhere in his paper, as components of other things. The works of Langston Hughes may be taught in a general course on American literature, not Afro-American literature. Slavery may be taught in a course on American history. I do not think that there is as much urgency in Africa to study Afro-American problems as there is in America to study African problems. Now, this may be the result of the American situation. Perhaps Americans felt isolated as a result of their own experience and, therefore, in the twentieth century wanted to get in on the act. So they took interest in such things as African studies and, of course, Afro-Americans wanted to identify themselves with Africa in the sixties.

I certainly appeal that the curriculum needs to be restructured to make students aware that African heritage extends beyond the boundaries of the continent, that it should include Afro-American history. As an instrument for bringing about this change I suggest the establishment in African universities of what one might call an *institute* or, if you like, *institute of Afro-American studies or diaspora studies*. (We can devise the term for it.) It seems to me that in this kind of institute, the teaching and the research should be much more coordinated, done on a much less piecemeal basis than it is at the moment.

Perhaps it is even more important for us in African universities to establish an institute of Afro-American studies than an institute of African studies, although these are proliferating in all African universities. We never hear of the "institute of English studies" in English universities; they have a Department of English Studies there. I am not sure whether an institute of French studies exists in French universities; maybe you have an institute of American studies in American universities. I do not know. But we have an Institute of African Studies. I have heard distinguished academics say that perhaps we should not have an institute of African studies in African universities, that perhaps the whole of the African university should be considered to be an "institute of African studies." The whole university should be engaged in the study of African affairs, and this kind of separate institute is unnecessary. Nevertheless, I certainly think that we need an institute of Afro-American studies as an instrument for coordinated teaching and research.

I did say that I was going to speak about this against the background of the constraints in which we have to operate in African universities. In our attempt to introduce all these new disciplines, these new departments, these institutes, and so on, we in African universities come up against a very narrow definition of relevance. A lot of people tell us what is relevant for us and, of course, we are now assisted by a lot of English and American experts who know what is relevant for us—what we need is African engineering, agriculture, and economics—and they do not see anything that we can call *liberal arts*. It seems to me that the kind of program of study I am talking about can generally be taught under the umbrella of liberal arts. But, I suspect, a lot of people will say this is not terribly relevant. Of course, we have the obligation to convince the educational planners (and not *just* the educational planners, but the government of our countries as well) that these things are relevant.

Research Materials

Professor Harris spoke at some length about the kinds of materials available in America. Although, of course, by some kind of agreement you may make some of these materials available to us, but the material is over there. American universities are very good at getting some of the materials that ought to be in Africa. Some of the best holdings in African literature are not to be found in African universities. The University of Texas in Austin has a lot. After I published my first book, I received a letter from out of the blue from an American university saying: "We understand you published a book. Would you like to sell your manuscript to us"? This kind of thing goes on. Americans are in the position to get many of the resource materials that we could use in African universities because they have the financial resources to get them. Also, perhaps Liberians have this kind of vision. I must give Americans the credit. They have the vision that they must get research materials, and perhaps we should start to build up these kinds of things. For all these reasons, it seems to me that this kind of thing will have to be done on America soil.

Professor Harris also mentioned the training of teachers. I agree that the training of teachers in the field is extremely important, just as research in the field is extremely important. But again, if I suggest the training of research assistants who would come and specialize in Afro-American studies, I will have to justify this to the planners, and the planners will have to justify it to the government, and funds for this kind of thing are very, very scarce; but I will come to this later.

First, we have neither the personnel nor the resources to do this kind of training within our African universities, so we will have to send our resources and potential teachers of these courses to you in the United States. This, of course, raises all sorts of problems. Another constraint includes problems in obtaining journals and books. Mr. James made the point yesterday that quite often we academics in Africa are hampered in all sorts of ways by the unavailability of those things. I am always filled with envy when I go to British or American universities and walk into the bookshop. You do not have to contend with the kind of foreign-exchange problem that we have to contend with to get all those journals and books. Even getting a subscription to a particular journal across, as Professor James pointed out yesterday, may be quite a difficult kind of enterprise. Also, we must bear in mind the status of research in African countries and African universities and the amount of funds devoted to it. I remember one year in the whole of the faculty of arts of Fourah Bay College, we only had Le 500—less than $500.00 for research. This is the kind of problem that we have to face. Despite the high cost of training our graduates in America, I guess the training will have to be done on American soil. We have to send them over to you. But are you in the best position to tell us how many dollars it costs to train a research assistant every year? I suspect it will be in the region of $6,000 or $7,000.

There is also the question of our own priorities. For instance, the government may tell us that our priorities do not include generating even this kind of link with Afro-America. Our priorities are agriculture, health, and so on. We will come back to this question of priorities as well. What I am suggesting is that it might be very difficult for us to generate these funds ourselves. So, do we have to fall back on the old donors? The Ford Foundation was mentioned. Do we have to fall back on Carnegie, the Ford Foundation, Rockefeller, Fulbright, all those things? Will this not be perpetuating the dependency that we have been talking about? Or are we going to tap internal sources? There must be lots of African tycoons. As Professor Dumbuya said yesterday, we know some of them, we know where they got their money. There must be lots of Afro-American tycoons. But are African tycoons renowned for their generosity toward the liberal arts? Are Afro-Americans? We may be able to devise a way of getting them interested. I will just mention one or two. Of course, we can always fall back on UNESCO. But let us take this burning question, the generation of the funds. Let me mention the role that has been played by various kinds of exchange schemes. I think Professor Harris mentioned some of them in his paper.

At Fourah Bay College, for instance, I hasten to say we also teach some aspects of Afro-American studies in our history and English departments, and so on. But we have had exchanges under the Phelps Stokes Foundation. For instance, some of our academics go to colleges in America and teach there for a while and do research; we do not have quite as many coming over here. And this is really significant because this kind of exchange, although it is meant to be an exchange, is not really an exchange, for it is a one-way exchange, and I wonder whether one can call a one-way exchange an exchange. We also have the same thing going on with students. We are supposed to send some of our students to American universities, and they are supposed to send some of theirs to us. The fact is that American students come to us quite often and few of our own students go over. This, again, has to do with all sorts of problems of ability to pay traveling costs, relieve salaries, and that sort of thing. We will have to pay the salaries of American colleagues coming to us. And given the salary structure (if you know how much I am paid at the University of Sierra Leone, for instance) you will never dream of coming there even to visit. We will not be able to pay the fees of our students if they go to those universities.

The Provision of Funds

How do we generate funds for this kind of exercise? I have already suggested that we have very little hope of getting it from African governments. Again, I want to see this in the context of the relationship which exists betwen African universities and African governments. It is different from what exists between American universities and the American government. Someone said some time ago that we have seen what African governments have done to the civil service, the judiciary, the military, and so on, but the actual test will be what they do to their own universities. Of course, you all know that once an African leader comes to power, he installs himself as chancellor of the university. They like being chancellors of these universities; they enjoy it. Soon the universities are in conflict with the government, and the politicians realize that it is not such an enjoyable thing to be chancellor of a university. But they install themselves as chancellors, and this is symbolic of the stranglehold that an African government can have on an African university. The government is about the only source of funds, and he who pays the piper calls the tune. Everything has to be justified to the government. When I go to a meeting of our planning and development committee, there is a representative of the government there. And as I have already suggested, if I want to go ahead with a program of African studies, I have to justify it to that representative or to the ministry of education. I will give you one small illustration. One of the research exercises we were going through in the University of Sierra Leone and Fourah Bay College was the compilation of a Creole-English dictionary, the first of such dictionaries from our own side. Because this involved a tremendous amount of money, particularly when it came to publication, we were to receive a portion of the funds from the ministry. I will not tell you how long it took us. I think we have just received the money, long after publication, and we had to get some loan from somewhere to pay costs in the meantime.

Another example. We were asked to institute a department of linguistics, a study of indigenous languages. We thought the money was forthcoming, so we went ahead and started teaching linguistics. Up to now we have not received the money. So, it seems the teaching of linguistics will have to be suspended.

The point I am making is that African universities are dependent on their governments for funds and, therefore, all these things—the new curriculum structure, the research projects, and so on, the new institutes which have to be set up—will have to be justified. And ultimately, it seems to me that decision makers have to be involved in the process and persuaded that the kind of awareness we are talking about—a black awareness, an awareness of the linkages, and an awareness of our relationship with Africans in the diaspora—is important and relevant. This is why again and again I keep coming to the theme of this seminar—a lot depends on political arrangements and political decisions. We have to get the politicians involved and persuaded that this is necessary. But I have already suggested that, in addition to persuading the government, mechanisms must also be devised for generating funds from nongovernmental African and Afro-American institutions to support this kind of development.

Research Emphases

Finally, I come to the kind of basic research that will have to be done. Professor Harris has mentioned quite a few things that have been done in other areas; however, from my own selfish point of view as a teacher of literature and so on, I would like to see emphasis placed on research on cultural matters. I know Dr. Dumbuya will say that one mentions cultural matters when one cannot find the term for other things, but I will illustrate what I mean.

Professor Harris has shown us his book, *Global Dimensions of the African Diaspora*. Scanning through the list of contributors and the topics, I see that there is emphasis on the historical. I also mention that in our department, Professor Jones and I jointly edited a journal called *Africa Today*. Volume nine of that journal is devoted to African-American relations, literary relations largely, the literary influences. I am interested in our literary relations, in our artistic relations or, if you like, in our cultural relations. I was at the opening ceremony of the Festival of African Culture (FESTAC). Afro-Americans attended and, I think, they had the largest contingent. They had a tremendous response from the audience. This is one of the things I think FESTAC achieved—if it did not achieve much more—bringing this kind of awareness of our relationship.

In cultural matters I would like to see more work done on the oral traditions, historical as well as literary oral traditions. How similar is Afro-American oral tradition to the African oral tradition, and how has one influenced the other? How can one say that the style of Afro-American writing has been determined by Afro-American historical experiences and by certain aspects of style in African oral literature? Afro-American music and art and its relationship to African music and art should also be examined.

I would like for us to pay more attention to black aesthetics. In Africa, we have been doing some work toward the emerging of an African aesthetic. One would like to see what work has been done on Afro-American aesthetics. What do black people consider to be beautiful, and how does this differ from what white people consider to be beautiful? Everyone tells us that for us, African plumpness is a sign of beauty. I do not know whether you have the corresponding thing in Afro-America. What exactly is the nature of black aesthetics? The question of identity has been raised again and again. During the discussion of the Liberian Experience, we heard so much about the identity crisis in Liberia. We also had, and still have, an identity crisis in Sierra Leone, as you had and perhaps still have an identity crisis in Afro-America. So, how do these relate? Well, these are some of the kinds of things one might also mention. But as Professor Harris has said, the list is by no means exhaustive. There will be all sorts of other research topics. But in order to do all this, we need to:

(1) encourage the establishment of centers of American/Afro-American studies (when I say American, I do not mean just North America, but about Brazil, as well, and the American diaspora in general);

(2) devise mechanisms for persuading governments and politicians that this kind of general exercise is necessary; and

(3) devise new mechanisms for generating funds from within Africa and Afro-America at the nongovernmental level to support this development.

Continuing Mechanisms for Discourse

Adelaide M. Cromwell

MOST of us who are old enough and experienced enough know that the most significant events rarely just happen—they must be planned.
The subtitle of this seminar, "From Dependency to Self-Reliance," was not chosen casually. But, then, even this title does not encompass all that we wish to imply. For in establishing the basis for this seminar, we knew that we Africans and Afro-Americans shared an earlier common independence as people of Africa who became separated under different but similar forms of dependency: slavery and colonization. Now, with the struggles for independence in the fifties and sixties in Africa and for civil rights in the United States behind us, we are again seeking the same destiny—complete self-reliance. Furthermore, we know that *nowhere*, either in Africa or in the States have we, as yet, achieved the complete self-reliance we seek. This fact alone is sobering and becomes the tie that binds us.

Self-reliance does not mean isolation or separation from those who surround us or those who might have formerly oppressed us. Self-reliance means *equality in negotiation*. To achieve self-reliance, it is necessary to acquire the commitment of many—the politician, the economist, the educator, the artist, the journalist, the soldier, the scholar, and the farmer. We cannot all do everything, but we can accept the responsibility of doing what we do well and consistently.

The distinguishing feature of our species—homo sapiens, (I guess that now sounds antifeminist)—is that we can *think* and *plan*. This seminar was convened to assemble thinkers and planners.

Since the very early days of our dependency, the major assumption underlying the justification for maintaining us in that condition was

115

that we were not supposed to be able to think for ourselves or plan for ourselves. The definitions, limitations, and solutions to our problems were always given to us by others. This was as true for Africans as for Afro-Americans. However, neither Africans nor Afro-Americans ever stopped thinking alone or in groups about their condition and what they could do to change it.

This seminar is but one in a long line of endeavors needed now more than ever because of the temptation and the danger in our thinking that we, as African people, can "do it alone," apart from one another: Nigerians apart from Senegalese, Senegalese apart from Kenyans, all Africans apart from those in the States and, even there, Bostonians apart from Chicagoans or those in Atlanta or those in Los Angeles. This must be changed. We must not forget our common ancestry nor the similarity of our historical and even contemporary condition.

Today, in January 1983, almost one hundred years after the Berlin Conference, we are again trying to determine how we can continue to know each other and plan jointly for ourselves on the basis of our interests and our knowledge. In 1969, in a volume I co-edited with Martin Kilson, *Apropos of Africa*, I tried to give briefly in the introduction, the short history of our earlier attempts to know each other:

> The period of a conscious search among Black Americans for an understanding of and identity with their African heritage began during the mid-1800's when there appeared the beginnings of a black American intelligentsia. With the end of the Civil War and the start of a measure of black social mobility within American society, this intelligentsia expanded the forms of its interests in their African heritage. In particular, there was an increasing concern for self-identity in a situation of social mobility towards the norms of a segregated American society. Such mobility necessarily rendered the black Americans' sense of self, of racial or cultural identity, ambivalent. In resolving this ambivalence the intellectual elements among Blacks turned to their African heritage in one form or another.
>
> Simultaneous with the Black American intelligentsia's confrontation with the white supremacist forms of American institutions which impelled their search for their African heritage, there was occurring in Africa itself the full colonization of the continent by European powers. Among other things, European colonization in Africa established patterns of racial segregation comparable to those founded in American society. In other words, colonization brought the black African into precisely the same type of relationships with white-dominated industrial society that Blacks in America, the Caribbean and South America were already experiencing. It, therefore, created the context within which the intelligentsia in both the old and new world black communities could identify their common needs and seek their amelioration. This was the starting point of what became known as Pan-Africanism.[1]

Now, it is difficult to state precisely when the first African-American saw his or her relationship to Africa or the need to communicate with Africans and/or the similarity in their respective conditions. Distance, language, and ideology combined to deter them. Nevertheless, the tie was never severed. In the early days of slavery, slaves often called themselves *Africans* and were so called by others. The earliest census of free blacks in Boston referred to them as *Africans*. In addition, blacks identified their earliest institutions as *African:* African Lodge 459 of the Masons, the first black fraternal order, and the Free African Society, forerunner of the African Methodist Episcopal Church, the first independently organized black church, as well as a series of African Free Schools.

But as a group, blacks in Africa and in the New World have always lacked the financial resources and the opportunities to communicate effectively with each other across the ocean. Nevertheless, the very fact that we, thirty-nine Africans from six countries and six Afro-Americans, are all here today in a group, albeit not much larger but certainly more representative than the first Pan-African Congress in 1900 in London (H. Sylvester Williams's congress of some thirty-odd delegates "mainly from England and the West Indies with a few colored North Americans"), indicates that we have not only sustained an interest but, fragile as it may be, it can still bring us together.

Where then do we go from here and how? As a veteran of a number of endeavors to pursue these goals, I feel we can and should learn from past experiences before we project a plan for the future.

Focusing on the American side, the side I know best, and thus not discussing the Society for African Culture in Paris, I wish to describe the only organization of black intellectuals that historically had any impact or had any track record, the American Negro Academy. Fortunately, Alfred A. Moss, Jr., has published an in-depth study of the academy entitled *The American Negro Academy, Voice of the Talented Tenth.*

The American Negro Academy was started almost 86 years ago on March 5, 1897, in Washington, D.C., by nine men who invited forty-six others to join them in forming the first black learned society to promote black culture and history and to answer the growing prevalent theories of white racists. Through annual meetings and published occasional papers and monographs, these few men struggled for thirty-one years to achieve their goals. From the beginning, the ties and relation to Africa were manifest in the structure and interests of the academy. Its founder and most distinguished member, Alexander Crummell, a New Yorker by birth and a graduate of Cambridge University, had matured as a clergyman and scholar during his years as a missionary and educator in Liberia. Crummell was the first president of the academy, followed by W. E. B. Du Bois, whose activities in and influence on the academy were not particularly notable. (I think this was largely due to the distance from Atlanta to Washington, D.C. Du Bois was in Atlanta, and it was probably as hard then to get money to travel from Washington to Atlanta as it is now to travel from Washington to Monrovia.) But as a distinguished scholar already committed to Africa, Du Bois's relation to the academy is important to remember today.

John Henry Smyth, the United States Minister to Liberia (1878–1885) was another early member. The academy had, from the first, distinguished Africans as corresponding members. Edward Wilmot Blyden, Sir Samuel Lewis, Samuel Coleridge Taylor, J. E. K. Aggrey, and Joseph Casely Hayford comprised the list.

Also, in the early days Crummell went to England and interested H. Sylvester Williams of Trinidad, originator of the first Pan-African Congress, and T. I. T. Thompson of Sierra Leone in what black Americans were doing, and they, in turn, formed the African Association of London.

Moss feels the academy died for several reasons: (1) lack of financial support, (2) lack of recognition by white scholars, (3) lack of appeal to issues of felt-importance to the average black (the folk as opposed to the intellectuals), and (4) a structural conflict that undercut its efforts to be a truly learned society. This conflict surfaced around the issue of membership, between those who were truly scholars, prepared to do scholarly work in the interest of the academy and those who were merely distinguished or influential personages. This polarity in membership qualifications confused the public image of the academy.

The post-World War I mood further weakened the organization because racism became more evident, thus making intellectuals seek other solutions—either a greater identification with their cultural roots, as expressed in the so-called Negro Renaissance, or in the desire to leave America and return to Africa, as expressed in writings and programs of Marcus Garvey.

So, after many learned discussions and the publication of twenty-three occasional papers, the academy died in 1928—unnoticed and unmourned. There is some evidence that in 1941 Du Bois tried unsuccessfully to revive the academy. Also, in 1969, the Black Academy of Arts and Letters was inaugurated at an impressive meeting in Boston; this group, albeit a distinguished membership, did little more than have notable social affairs and vote some obviously important blacks into a now defunct Hall of Fame.

Why then am I recounting this saga of an organization of great importance and some accomplishments which no longer exists? I do so because I believe that the fact it ever existed and to some extent flourished proves an important point: namely, the capabilities of black intellectuals to reach out and communicate with each other in the States and in Africa. What has been done is, therefore, quite possible to repeat.

The failure of the academy to survive did not stem from the lack of knowledge of its members or even from their lack of education. The academy failed because of the lack of funds and the lack of recognition by the larger society and because it did not face the issues that concerned the average black person. The academy cannot be faulted for the lack of recognition by the larger society, for we know well the subtle ways the larger society or the larger world has of recognizing and ignoring us—sometimes especially when we are onto a good thing—on the way to a breakthrough for self-reliance.

But equally important, in my opinion, in the academy's failure was the lack of a permanent institutional base—they were forced to meet in someone's living room or some other organization's borrowed rooms. Today, with the many universities in Africa and in the United States at predominantly black colleges, there is certainly the possibility of having an organizational base on which could be sustained activities to recruit and stimulate the intellectual potential of blacks.

It is, therefore, I think, high time for African universities and American universities—those predominantly black or those with a commitment to Afro-American studies—working in cooperation, to address the question of making more visible and more meaningful the "Dynamics of the African/Afro-American Connection."

To accomplish this, it will be necessary to expand the library resources in this area, enrich the archives, ever mindful of the meager and fast-disappearing sources of documentation of oral history, family histories, and institutional histories and, of course, to make our curricular offerings more relevant. Beyond that, however, I am thinking of the university, as academe, as a community of scholars where people convene to learn—to discuss, to dispute, to share ideas, and to do research—as a place where there can be periodic meetings with a larger constituency and where publishable papers are written and then circulated.

Indeed, I feel, we could do no better than following much of the academy format but avoiding its pitfalls and especially strengthening it by providing an institutional base—a permanent one or a regional one in rotation. A by-product of this movement would be the strengthening of institutional alliances among the many institutions in Africa, the Caribbean, and the United States.

During this seminar there has been much talk of a global perspective on the African/Afro-American Connection. Irrespective of how one might argue this relationship, it is also clear that there is a need for improved communication and better understanding among most of the people on this planet. From time to time, this has high priority for a given government or a given group. As an illustration of that, the United States Information Agency (USIA), with which I am associated as a member of the Board of Foreign Scholarships, has been developing programs to achieve goals similar to those of the workshop held in Boston in 1981 and the seminar here in 1983. The program within the United States Information Agency is designed to "bridge the chasm of misunderstanding between the United States and the Europeans," a so-called trans-Atlantic dialogue on the value of mutual understanding. Accordingly, five American scholars will meet this January with ten European scholars from Belgium, Germany, Iceland, Italy, The Netherlands, Sweden, and from the United States in much the same fashion as we conducted our workshop session in Boston in the spring of 1981, two years earlier! That is, without prepared papers as such, they will explore through informal discussions the extent to which the value assumptions of the program of international academic exchange may have been affected by changes in values.

These participants will have "as their ultimate purpose the recollecting and reactivating of common values which earlier (1949) were taken for granted as a basis of mutual understanding across the boundaries of nations, peoples, and cultures and secondly, to find out which of these values may have been weakened or rejected and which continue as binding commitments and, therefore, to envisage potential adjustments in the broad policies of academic exchange."

After this preliminary meeting, a larger international conference more or less comparable to our meeting here will be convened in Europe to discuss the subject of common values in the context of academic exchange and to produce a public statement on the matter.

This trans-Atlantic dialogue is admittedly more focused in its goal than our efforts have been, in that it will address the questions of academic exchange exclusively; nevertheless, there is a strong similarity between their endeavors and ours, because academic exchanges are merely one form of communication, and to be effective, they must rest on a common set of values and assumptions. Our meetings have also been designed to explore ways of communicating and articulating common values and assumptions, which the passage of time and diversity of experience may have weakened.

One other example, briefly, to test the minds of current thinking (also being considered but not yet implemented by USIA) is to create a a center to study those political and economic issues that influence the relationship between the United States and Africa; that is, questions of development, trade, international finance, debt, sources and uses of energy, commodities, population, urbanization, agriculture, and land usage. These are all considered to be basic to the relationship between the United States and African countries and as on-going and potentially volatile. With one or two exceptions, it does not take much imagination to note that many of these issues are equally relevant as concerns between the American government and its black citizens— viz., development, urbanization, agriculture, uses of energies are clearly of special concern to black Americans.

Should this particular program be implemented, therefore, it is important that it relate to a predominantly black institution and that black Americans as well as Africans be invited to participate in its deliberations. In order to participate meaningfully as Africans or as black Americans we need to be exposed to the kind of enrichment and dialogue such as this seminar has offered. In the fall of 1983, Boston University, Harvard University, and the Massachusetts Institute of Technology, as a consortium, were awarded a one-year grant to implement this idea.

In conclusion, then, we can see that in participating in the discussions of this seminar, we are not pioneers. We have a distinguished legacy, and we are not alone on the planet or in a particular position of isolation in wanting to communicate and reach common values for all people.

However, as Africans and Afro-Americans we must also have our own respective agenda, relevant to our needs and period of history. We must define ourselves and understand in what ways we can and must help each other. The issues are complex: we are an extremely diverse people—shared oppression or similar pigmentation may be the bottom line, but diverse experiences, even different goals, must be understood and acknowledged.

To me, the existence of universities in Africa as independent institutions is the key to our situation. The university provides the component to our search for self-reliance. It can be a source of strength and enrichment.

It is perhaps not inappropriate to note that African universities, as meaningful institutions within their own countries and for the continent as a whole, may have to alter somewhat the rigidly Western mold into which they were historically cast and see the necessity for playing an important identifiable role in strengthening the ties between Africans on the continent and Africans abroad. The University of Liberia, as an outgrowth of Liberia College, which was founded in 1862 as the first independent institution of higher learning for blacks in Sub-Saharan Africa, has been the appropriate place to start this dialogue in Africa.

Many predominantly black institutions in the United States have a long record of association with Africa. Lincoln University in Pennsylvania started in 1854 as Ashmum Institute for the training of missionaries for Africa and is known more recently in this century as the alma mater of many prominent Africans. However, Howard University, by its strategic location in Washington, D.C., and as the first federally sponsored institution for higher learning for blacks in the United States, having had a distinguished faculty (two, Professor Kelly Miller and Dr. Alain Locke, were members of the American Negro Academy) and with perhaps the most extensive curriculum of any black institution, has been a leader in exploring the issues and problems of blacks in the diaspora.

Now is the time for a gathering in—for universities in Africa and abroad to address the subjects discussed in this seminar, not merely in the form of course offerings but as a basis for research, publications, and further dialogue. Let us hope they accept this challenge.

I think this seminar will have historic significance—more of us have met more of us, have learned more about all of us, but this can only be the beginning of the process to meet the responsibilities inherited from the past—from our ancestors.

I thank you for coming; I thank the University of Liberia especially and also the University of Sierra Leone and Boston University, the Ford Foundation, the United States Educational and Cultural Foundation, and the American Ambassador for making this seminar possible. But the real task and responsibility for moving forward with this experience is like the Kingdom of God: it is within each of us. May we have the strength to achieve it.

NOTE

1. Adelaide Cromwell Hill and Martin Kilson, eds., *Apropos of Africa* (London: Frank Cass and Co., 1969), xiii–xiv.

Response

Amos Sawyer

P ROFESSOR Cromwell's presentation has provided the historical connection between what we have done in this seminar and the past. It has also awakened a great feeling of solidarity and spirituality with the past efforts of black people to define themselves and determine for themselves their destiny. I wish her presentation had not been the concluding presentation but the introductory one, setting the stage for the presentations of Professor Skinner and others.

The significance of the seminar on the African/Afro-American Connection has been discussed throughout this seminar and has been re-emphasized by Dr. Cromwell as we close. By discussing at length the experience of the American Negro Academy, she has shown the practical problems that may face us as we attempt to establish a mechanism for discourse.

Dr. Cromwell did not intend to leave the impression that the American Negro Academy was the only mechanism linking black people. We may point with satisfaction to the Pan-African congresses, which although plagued with financial problems, like the Negro Academy, concerned themselves with issues of vital importance to all classes of black people. Most important is the fact that the congresses were concerned with issues from which action-oriented programs were produced. This should be an important point of emphasis in our current endeavor. Discourse must seek not only to bridge the communication gap and strengthen our sense of identity and destiny or to provide a major contribution to the advancement of our knowledge of ourselves. The discourses we now undertake should also enable us eventually to develop a strategy for self-reliance and self-actualization. Furthermore, we must be able to develop a mechanism to operationalize that strategy.

A vital part of this enterprise has to do with our preparedness to develop, at the appropriate time, a strategy for influencing governments in Africa and the Americas to implement programs leading to self-reliance. If, eventually, this objective is to be incorporated into the long-range planning of our discourse, it will be important to emphasize, from the start, that all sectors of the black community must be represented in our discourse.

Another vital element is the creation of a mechanism for discourse in our universities. While our universities as institutions for the making and dispensing of knowledge "provide the component to our search," as Dr. Cromwell says, they must also be the point of convergence of the various elements in the black experience. They must be the crucible for synthesis. And so, for these purposes, while they realize themselves as independent institutions, they must facilitate the interdependency of the various segments of the black experience and continually monitor and describe the ever-changing global context of which we are all a part.

Summary and Recommendations

Patrick L. N. Seyon

THIS seminar is another manifestation of the growing concern black scholars have for the "black dilemma" in a world system that is polarized between the scientific-technologically advanced and prosperous nations, on the one hand, and the poor nations (most of which are black and the majority of the twenty-three poorest nations are in Africa) on the other hand. It is a world system in which "Race" (with a capital R but often pronounced without notice that it is a capital R) has been and continues to be the "invisible hand" directing the affairs and apparent destiny of black peoples the world over. The most critical aspects of the "black dilemma" are not, in my view, (1) that black peoples within the world system are comparatively economically poor and politically weak vis-à-vis their white counterparts, important as this may be; (2) that they have no significant role in and/or control over the means of production; (3) that they are not part of the "power elite" that make the critical decisions in both the national and international arenas; (4) that they are conditioned psychologically and intellectually to conceive and perceive of themselves as their oppressors and suppressors have taught them (I am refering to the process of intellectual and cultural colonization for which a real revolution is needed); or (5) that they lack a significant amount of scientific and technological knowledge to ameliorate their conditions. The most critical aspect of the "black dilemma" is black peoples' level of consciousness of their collective condition in the world system. It is one's consciousness of one's condition that leads to action which can alter a given condition in one's favor. While Jews everywhere are highly conscious of their historical oppression and are determined never to have it occur in any form or shape, blacks have not now or in the recent past demonstrated a similar level of consciousness regarding their condition.

Even though there was a high level of black consciousness stirred up by the Pan-African movement at the close of the nineteenth century and the beginning of the twentieth century, this consciousness has significantly decreased in the second half of the twentieth century as result of a number of factors, chief among them being the rise of the nation-state and economic rights among black Americans. But blacks must not lose sight of the fact that the nation-states of Africa and the Caribbean are creations of imperialist powers that have vested interests in them through transnational corporations—the Africans and Caribbeans act as their agents and other international finance capital arrangements manipulate and control them. It is an open secret now in Africa, for example, that sometimes when a military coup d'état is staged to liberate the suffering masses, improve their standard of living, and stop corruption, it turns out that it is the imperialist powers and their allies who benefit.

During the past few days the discussions have focused attention on and sensitized us to the marginality of the black peoples in the world system. Our level of productivity, trade, and capital formation attest to this marginality. This raises the most important question from our deliberations: How can we influence the world system so as to alter our marginal role within it? The answer is not withdrawal, because we are too weak to withdraw and survive. The answer also is not to try to negotiate favorable conditions when the oppressors know that a change in the relation spells trouble for them. In a small way, there are things we can do internally that may force a favorable response from the system. Among others, these include improving our efficiency in management and production, eliminating corruption, and militantly refusing to be corrupted, using black expertise as opposed to white, and removing the trade barriers set up by our colonial masters so as to create a larger market.

This seminar has taken a significant first step in bringing together black scholars who are sufficiently conscious of the "black dilemma" to sit down and bang heads. You know one important aspect of the "black dilemma" is that black people do not talk to each other (the white folks call it consultation). If we do not talk to each other, how can we plan common strategy? If we cannot sit down and talk, how can we find solutions to our common problems? In this connection, I want to pay a special tribute to Dr. Adelaide Cromwell of Boston University and Dr. Mary Antoinette Brown Sherman of the University of Liberia for their initiatives and efforts in making this seminar possible.

Epilogue

Patrick L. N. Seyon and Herschelle S. Challenor

E IGHTY-THREE years after the first Pan-African Congress in 1900, thirty-nine Africans and six Afro-Americans met at the University of Liberia for the dual purpose of assessing their present condition and of developing a means of improving communications between Africans on the continent and those in the diaspora.

The University of Liberia, an outgrowth of Liberia College founded in 1892, was selected as the venue for this encounter not only because of its antecedents as the first independent institution of higher learning for blacks in Sub-Saharan Africa, but also because Liberia, as Africa's first independent nation, dramatized both the significance and the complexity of the African/Afro-American interaction. As indicated by Dr. Sherman and Dr. Caine, tension between Western, specifically American and British, ideas and African cultural values has been a perennial factor in the political evolution of Liberia.

That a conference on the African/Afro-American Connection took place in Liberia at all, so soon after the decisive rejection of Americo-Liberian overlordship on April 12, 1980, is in itself remarkable. This conference should be seen, therefore, as a tribute to the Liberian people and as a demonstration that the umbilical linkage between continental and New World Africans transcends political differences.

The seminar on the "Dynamics of the African/Afro-American Connection: From Dependency to Self-Reliance" recognized that historically Africa and its peoples had been objects of world, and essentially European, economic and political forces. Skinner and Mazrui each sketched four roughly corresponding historical stages, the first being the period from the sixteenth to the eighteenth century, comprising the discovery of the New World and the subsequent related European quest for African slave labor to develop it. This was followed by the

127

abolitionist period in the nineteenth century, which corresponded to the European realization that wage labor was more cost effective than slave labor and that Africa contained products of greater economic significance to Europe. This realization led to the imposition of colonial rule in Africa, a process which coincided with the "repatriation" of black American freedmen to Liberia and the British relocation of black poor from England, blacks from Nova Scotia, and slaves liberated on the high seas to Sierra Leone. By the late eighteenth century, we enter a third period, which encompassed both the beginning of the European exploitation of the mineral wealth in South Africa and other parts of the continent, and the first, in 1900, of what would be a series of Pan-African congresses. Finally, there is the contemporary period, characterized by the attainment of national sovereignty by most of the nations of Africa and the English-speaking Caribbean and the increased involvement of black Americans in economic and political ventures in Africa.

The key points discussed at the seminar were the persistence of contacts between continental and trans-Atlantic Africans and the salient role of the English language and the leading "Anglo-Saxon" state in influencing the fate of African peoples.

Throughout these four periods, contacts between New World and continental Africans were identified. Historically, the black church and the black colleges operated as bridging institutions that brought these two groups of African peoples together.

A constant reality has been that Europeans/whites have tended to mediate the relationships between continental and trans-Atlantic African peoples. Realizing that contacts between black freedmen and slaves or dependent peoples were potentially volatile, the United States government delayed recognition of Haiti and Liberia until after the emancipation of the slaves in 1865. Similarly, European colonial governments discouraged black American missionary activities in southern Africa, particularly after the Chilembwe uprising in then Nyasaland in the early twentieth century.

Black response to such constraining activities varied. Dr. Nicol pointed to the "dis-Africanization" of blacks in the United States beginning around 1825, which coincided with the establishment of the American Colonization Society. Resisting efforts once again to treat them as expendable commodities to serve white interests, American blacks, who heretofore incorporated the name *African* in the titles of many of their churches and social institutions, removed this appellation and began to insist on their rights as U.S. citizens.

The anglophone connection, Dr. Mazrui pointed out, has been decisive in the history of African peoples. Great Britain was the principal colonizer of both Africa and the United States and emerged as the leading power in the Caribbean. Britain and the United States established the two "sanctuary" states of Liberia and Sierra Leone in the mid-nineteenth century. Leaders of the Pan-African movement, such as H. Sylvester Williams, George Padmore, W. E. B. Du Bois, and Marcus Garvey, came from the United States and the English-speaking Caribbean. These men interacted in later years with Kwame Nkrumah, Jomo Kenyatta, and Hastings Kamuzu Banda, all from British African colonies.

The French did create Libreville for rescued slaves; Blaise Diagne did attend the Pan-African Congress in 1914, and Aimé Césaire, Léon Damas, and Léopold Sédar Senghor did launch the *Négritude* movement. However, the francophone African and Antillean response to European rule was principally cultural, as opposed to the more political and nationalist orientation of anglophone blacks. Moreover, since the last stage of decolonization on the Africa continent will take place in Namibia and South Africa, where the United Kingdom and the United States remain the major external economic partners and where English-speaking Africans will wage the liberation struggle, the primacy of "anglodom" in the African world is likely to continue in the future.

If there were two underlying themes, there remained two unanswered questions. First, how can continental and diasporan Africans achieve sufficient economic security so that they can exercise political power at home and genuine independence in international affairs? Second, despite the apparent symbiotic relationship between Afro-Americans and local Africans in Liberia, even after the events of 1980, will greater Afro-American involvement in the continent lead to the "Liberianization" of Africa, that is, the introduction of a potentially conflictual presumptive elite? A corollary to that question is what problems are caused by the fact that Afro-Americans are "an oppressed minority in a privileged state"? In short, will it be culture, race, and a shared historical experience, or rather national boundaries and citizenship that will determine the primordial identities in the African world?

The Liberia Declaration approved by the seminar stated *inter alia*, "that neither the ravages of history nor the distance of geography have as yet extinguished the ambition to restore deeper contact between Africa and its wider frontiers across the seas. . . . That we recognize the duality of our existence as related to citizenship and heritage. However, we believe that our fundamental Africanity transcends territorial boundaries." Implicitly accepting the superordination of cultural, racial, and experiential affinities, the seminar decided to convene another meeting on inter-African and diasporan relations in

Africa within two years. This meeting would be more representative and involve persons from the Caribbean and both French- and English-speaking Africa. An interim secretariat, composed of the University of Liberia and Boston and Howard universities in the United States, was charged with preparing such a meeting.

However, two years after the seminar, dramatic changes in Liberia, on the African continent, and in the United States have impeded the realization of these stated goals. The most devastating blow was the militarization of the University of Liberia in August 1984. Following the issuance of two statements by the university calling for the release of, or minimally a fair trial for, Professor Amos Sawyer, who had been detained by the government for "security reasons," the Liberian army routed the campus, closed the university, and dismissed the entire adminstration and senior faculty. This removal of university President Mary Antoinette Brown Sherman and Vice-President Patrick Seyon and the arrest of Professor Amos Sawyer, the three main Liberian coordinators of the seminar, effectively denied them the base so essential for carrying out the charge the seminar gave to them.

An underlying suggestion of the seminar, articulated by Dr. Cromwell, that "the existence of universities in Africa as independent institutions is the key to our situation" and that they provide "the component to our search for self-reliance," proved to be premature. Over the past five years, several countries, including Nigeria, Kenya, Ivory Coast, Sierra Leone, and Benin have closed, or imposed restrictions on, their universities. The university, and intellectuals generally, remain vulnerable to the political whims of politicians and to the fragility of the nation-state in Africa. Free speech and academic freedom have yet to be assured. The desire expressed by Dr. Harris, to see the expansion of Afro-American/diaspora studies at African universities, may have to await the consolidation of greater independence for the university itself.

Two other events, the famine and economic crisis that crippled Africa in 1983–1985 and the 1984 reelection of President Reagan by an overwhelming majority in the United States, narrowed the prospects for a greater measure of political influence and economic prosperity for African peoples on both sides of the Atlantic. The problems of African economic dependency highlighted by Dr. Johnson have become more acute. Moreover, Nigeria, the suggested venue for the 1985 seminar, inevitably had its priorities altered as a consequence of the economic reversal resulting from the world oil glut.

The African famine dramatized for the world the seriousness of the structural economic crisis facing that continent. Impaled on the trident of debt, deterioration of terms of trade, and declining agricultural productivity, many African countries have had to take extreme belt-tightening measures. Indeed, the imposition of cutbacks on post-secondary education by certain states in order to avoid problems caused by skilled manpower surpluses in stagnating economies may further weaken universities in the years ahead.

The postseminar changes suggest that economic and political constraints continue to influence the African/Afro-American Connection. It remains to be seen whether we will be neutralized by these forces, or reinforce our determination to move from dependency to self-reliance precisely because of them.

Appendixes
Contributors
Index

Appendix A

The Liberia Declaration:
A Statement of the Symposium on
the Dynamics of the African/Afro-American Connection
Monrovia, January 10–15, 1983

We, the participants at this International and Inter-African Symposium, meeting in Monrovia, Liberia, from January 10 to 15, 1983, to discuss the "Dynamics of the African/Afro-American Connection: From Dependency to Self-Reliance," do hereby affirm the following propositions:

THAT dignified identity is the birthright of every people.

THAT by sharing ancestry and the experience of centuries of exploitation, the sons and daughters of Africa share identity as a people wherever they may be.

THAT neither the ravages of history nor the distances of geography have as yet extinguished the ambition to restore deeper contact between Africa and its wider frontiers across the seas.

THAT what the slave trade and the imperial scramble put asunder, let the Africans themselves, wherever they may be, put back together.

THAT we recognize the duality of our existence as related to citizenship and heritage. However, we believe that our fundamental Africanity transcends territorial boundaries.

THAT the twentieth century is the century of Pan-Africanism and the struggle to transcend dependency and exploitation.

THAT the time has come to institutionalize more effectively the quest for a deeper re-union between Africa and her diaspora in time for the new dawn in the year 2000.

In pursuit of that goal, this seminar proposes the establishment of an association for the purpose of advancing the cause of Pan-Africanism and the attainment of African liberation, decolonization, and self-reliance, and calls upon all African peoples to take resolute action in support of these objectives.

Historical Context

The present economic, political, and social situation of African peoples is but one stage of a historically conditioned process directly related to the emergence and the development of the modern world order. Over the past four hundred years in particular, African people have engaged in a collective struggle to liberate themselves from economic exploitation, social and political domination, and the persisting patterns of power and privilege based on racism, slavery, and imperialism.

The fight for the freedom of African peoples continues and requires new and more vigorous mechanisms and strategies for fundamental change. Facing us today are the equally brutal problems of underdevelopment and poverty,

135

dependency, race, and class inequality, which are global in scope. Yet to confront these issues there is a need for African peoples to redefine and reinterpret their realities, to take an honest look at their internal contradictions and institute constructive programs to eradicate poverty and social inequality, to appreciate the historical basis of their resilience and survival, and to build on these strengths.

The need for cooperation among African peoples is imperative. This must, be done while recognizing that African peoples belong to different nation-states and reside in various parts of the world. Fundamental, however, is the need to retain the perspective that our problems and conditions transcend geographical and political boundaries, they are global in nature and must be analyzed critically and dealt with on this level.

Through our collective efforts, African peoples of the continent and those of the dispersed communities and nations throughout the world can help create a more equitable and just world order for all people.

Short-term Goals

(1) THAT another meeting on inter-African and diaspora relations be held within two years in another African country.

(2) THAT at such a meeting the idea of forming a continuing association of inter-African and diaspora relations be explored.

(3) THAT prior explorations be made about the possibility of linking the proposed association with the Howard University-based and UNESCO-sponsored *Diaspora Newsletter,* which is about to be launched.

(4) THAT explorations also be made into the possibility of linking the proposed association with a regular journal of inter-African and diaspora studies.

(5) THAT, in the meantime, a joint interim secretariat consisting of the University of Liberia and Howard and Boston universities be formed with a mandate to seek funding and prepare for the next meeting on inter-African and diaspora relations.

(6) THAT the joint interim secretariat should also explore the involvement of peoples of African ancestry in the Caribbean, and Americas, Europe, and elsewhere.

(7) THAT all efforts be undertaken immediately to strengthen existing linkages between Africa and its diaspora, including academic and professional links, closer diplomatic ties, cultural cooperation, and other areas of inter-African and diaspora relations.

(8) THAT greater information be disseminated *in* the African world *about* the African world.

(9) THAT the proposed international association of inter-African and diaspora relations should explore areas of cooperation with other relevant regional and international organizations.

(10) THAT the association should seek formal status as a nongovernmental organization from the Organization of African Unity, the Organization of American States, and the League of Arab States with agencies of the United Nations system.

Long-Term Goals

(1) THAT there is an urgent need for peoples of Africa and of African ancestry to change their orientation, recognize their own potentialities as a people, and make themselves the centerpiece of their own destiny.

(2) THAT African peoples should design a new development strategy which draws mainly upon their own skills and resources, as they pursue self-reliance and better standards of living.

(3) THAT, in this regard, Africa and its diaspora must recognize that a new concept of unity can only be achieved if mini-sovereignty and subnationalism are subordinated to wider purposes.

(4) THAT those wider purposes require a re-ordering of African priorities in the light of the contemporary African condition and the historical experiences of African peoples.

(5) THAT the African world should implement this new strategy in full recognition of the hostile international environment and the adverse global forces which seek to dilute and weaken the African dimension in world affairs.

(6) THAT there is an urgent need to pull together the human and material resources of African peoples and mobilize their skills in pursuit of common development objectives and self-reliance.

(7) THAT there should be sustained efforts to improve the performance of African peoples, reduce inefficiency, and enhance their productive and creative skills.

(8) THAT linkages be strengthened among African peoples in pursuit of their shared goals of dignity, political liberation, cultural authenticity and economic advancement.

Mechanism

Having agreed that a permanent organization be set up to pursue the above objectives and advance the cause of Pan-Africanism it is hereby recommended:

(1) That the organization should meet every two years and that the next meeting should be convened on the African continent.

(2) That every effort should be made before the next general meeting to ensure that a much wider spectrum of all African peoples is represented at the said meeting.

(3) That the organization should establish permanent headquarters on the African continent.

Appendix B

Summary of Discussions and Workshops

Following each session, there was an opportunity for comments and questions from the audience. Interestingly, the same individuals attended several sessions of the seminar. Also, the same concerns were voiced over and over again.

The comments and questions were, for the most part, in three broad areas: economic development, Pan-Africanism, and the future. Although the formal papers stressed the comparability between Africans and Afro-Americans, having the seminar in Africa tended to direct the discussion to points more relevant to Africa.

Economic Development

From the African perspective, being in debt is worse than merely being dependent. Africans can be more self-reliant if they restrict what they consume to what they really need. They should not spend money on what is not needed and then have to beg for what is needed.

This self-sufficiency has to be achieved within a global context, that is, with an appreciation of the inevitability of some interdependency. But self-reliance should be sought regionally rather than country by country. There must be greater intra-Africa trade based on African raw materials.

Being self-sufficient economically means eliminating the psychological and intellectual dependency, which is affected by the type and level of education Africans receive.

Participants raised two major questions about economic development. First, will African people choose between dependency and poverty? To choose poverty, there must be knowledge of how to use local resources, especially agricultural resources. It makes no sense to spend millions importing rice to Africa. However, disengagement from the capitalist world will not solve Africa's economic problems.

Second, is there not a contradiction and paradox in advocating self-reliance and simultaneously seeking a substantial increase in foreign aid? Yet, foreign aid has become a major profit-making vehicle for multinational companies. But Africa should not look to the Western world for salvation. Africans should refuse inappropriate aid or loans for projects that have little priority in terms of their own development.

Power in the twenty-first century will be so dispersed that the United States will have to negotiate for what it needs, but the United States does not accept the notion that its security depends on the economic growth of the Third World. Now that oil is no longer as useful a weapon as it once was, the debt owed international lending agencies should be used as a weapon in economic development.

Afro-Americans should use their political power within the United States to influence policy toward Africa just as Americans did in responding to the needs of their allies after World War II.

Pan-Africanism

Participants agreed that we should not succumb to a doom theory nor should we take the present division of Africa as permanent. Rather, we should reexamine the positions of earlier thinkers such as Nkrumah, Blyden, and Tubman to redefine Pan-Africanism in modern terms. Specific aspects of the Pan-African movement should be remembered, such as the role of Ethiopia in the Italian invasion.

Participants expressed the importance of coming to terms with the on-going polarization of Africa by the great powers. A substantial portion of Africa is in the midst of internal warfare, thus creating the need for millions to be spent on refugees. How should Africans and Afro-Americans view the socialist bloc? How does the Organization of African Unity affect Pan-Africanism, since blacks in the diaspora are not represented in that body?

What of the Future?

Participants raised several questions about the future. An overarching question is: How can the ideas and issues discussed in this seminar be brought to average citizens, to involve them in the dynamics of the relationship between Africans and Afro-Americans? Questions of on-going significance included:

How can blacks from other areas of the diaspora, such as Brazil and the Caribbean, be integrated into this move for solidarity?

What do we know about Africans who have emigrated to the Muslim areas of the world?

Has language, viz., English or French, been a way of perpetuating our dependency? Perhaps efforts should be made to identify and use one dominant non-African language and as a goal for each country one indigenous African language and one foreign African language.

Finally, participants agreed that Africans and Afro-Americans need to stress the democratic ideal of a society in any form—liberal, African, or in combination. In addition, African countries should establish a center where research can be collected to explore ways in which we must face the future of the twenty-first century.

Workshops

Group One.

Group one summarized and agreed upon four major issues:

(1) There is a need for scholarly commitment by politicians.
(2) Africans and Americans must break their economic dependency. Nigeria was cited as an example.
(3) Pan-Africanism must be perceived as an ideological matter.
(4) Recognition must be given to the need for personal relationships in institutional decisions.

Group Two.

Group two discussed the issue of Pan-Africanism and raised the question: Has Pan-Africanism achieved its goals? The group identified three Pan-African goals:

(1) The Pan-African movement, including the diaspora, should be revitalized.
(2) Organization of African Unity states should forge stronger links with the rest of the world.
(3) Exchanges among Afro-American scholars should be vigorously promoted.

Group Three.

Group three discussed a variety of topics and arrived at four decisions:

(1) Black Americans must identify as American.
(2) Africans must perceive themselves first as African.
(3) All types of communication between Africans and Afro-Americans must be developed.
(4) Afro-Americans and Africans must publicly advocate each other's cause.

Group Four.

The issue of culture dominated this group's discussion. The group agreed upon two issues:

(1) Culture was broadly defined in terms of education and communication.
(2) African studies programs should be intensified and exchange programs should be established.

Finally, participants agreed that in union there is strength.

Appendix C

Workshop and Seminar Participants

Boston University Workshop Participants

Herschelle S. Challenor
UNESCO
Washington, D.C. 20006

Adelaide M. Cromwell
Department of Afro-American
  Studies and Sociology
Boston University
Boston, MA 02215

E. U. Essien-Udom
Department of Political Science
University of Ibadan
Ibadan, Nigeria

James Lowell Gibbs, Jr.
Department of Anthropology
Stanford University
Stanford, CA 94305

Roy A. Glasgow
Department of History and Afro-
  American Studies
Boston University
Boston, MA 02215

Ruth Simms Hamilton
Department of Sociology
Michigan State University
201 Berkey Hall
East Lansing, MI 48823

Joseph E. Harris
Department of History
Howard University
Washington, D.C. 20059

Nathaniel Huggins
Department of Afro-American
  Studies
Harvard University
W. E. B. Du Bois Institute
Cambridge, MA 02138

Willard R. Johnson
Department of Political Science
Massachusetts Institute of
  Technology
Cambridge, MA 02139

Tony Martin
Black Studies Department
Wellesley College
Wellesley, MA 02181

Micere M. Githae Mugo
Dean, Faculty of Arts
University of Nairobi
Nairobi, Kenya

Davidson Nicol
Former Director
United Nations Center for Training
  and Research

Pearl T. Robinson
Department of Political Science
Tufts University
Medford, MA 02155

Amos Sawyer
Dean, Liberia College
Monrovia, Liberia

Elliott P. Skinner
Department of Anthropology
Columbia University
New York, NY 10027

Akintola J. G. Wyse
Department of History
Southern University
Baton Rouge, LA 70813

Monrovia, Liberia Seminar Participants

Ghana

J. K. Fynn
Department of History
University of Ghana
Legon

Isaac Obeng-Quaindoo
School of Journalism and
   Communication
University of Ghana
Legon

Ivory Coast

Emily Dukho
Department of Literature
University of Abidjan
Abidjan

Emmanuel Mensah
Researcher, Institute of Applied
   Linguistics
University of Abidjan
Abidjan

Denis Zunon
Lecturer, Department of
   Management
College of Economics
University of Abidjan
Abidjan

Liberia

Kenneth Y. Best
Managing Director
The Daily Observer Corporation
Monrovia

Bill Frank Enoayi
Publisher/Editor
African Image
Paynesville

Evelyn White Kandakai
Dean of Academic Affairs
Cuttington University College
Suacoco

Christian E. Baker
President
Baker Homegrown Poultry
   Farms, Inc.
P. O. Box 1180
Monrovia

Theodora Ward Jackson
Dean, W. V. S. Tubman Teachers
   College
University of Liberia
Monrovia

G. Flamma Sherman
Former Ambassador of Liberia to
   Ghana and Former Minister of
   Education
Monrovia

A. Benedict Weeks
Managing Director
Auriole Enterprises, Inc.
P. O. Box 1564
Monrovia

John T. Woods
Development Consultants
P. O. Box 3624
Carey Street
Monrovia

Henry W. Yaidoo
Dean, College of Business and Public
   Administration
University of Liberia
Monrovia

Nigeria

M. Bassey Ate
Research Fellow
Institute of International Affairs
G. P. O. Box 1727
Lagos

Adekunle Ajala
Research Fellow
Institute of International Affairs
G. P. O. Box 1727
Lagos

U. Joy Ogwu
Research Fellow
Institute of International Affairs
G. P. O. Box 1727
Lagos

Senegal

Marieme Sy
Department of English
University of Dakar
Dakar

Sierra Leone

M. O. Cole
Deputy Permanent Secretary
Ministry of Foreign Affairs
Freetown

Moses B. Dumbuya
Lecturer, Department of Sociology
Fourah Bay College
University of Sierra Leone
Freetown

His Excellency Ernest Eastman
Secretary-General, Mano River Union
P. M. Bag 133
Freetown

Mohammed J. Tunis
Acting Director-General
Mass Media Services
Ministry of Information and
 Broadcasting
Freetown

Chairpersons and Rapporteurs

Cecelia Bull
Director of Continuing Education
University of Liberia
Monrovia

Herschelle S. Challenor
UNESCO
Washington, D.C.

Abraham L. James
Associate Professor of Political Science
University of Liberia
Monrovia

Al-Hassan Conteh
Assistant Professor of Demography
University of Liberia
Monrovia

Lumumba Kasongo
Assistant Professor of Political Science
University of Liberia
Monrovia

Althea Mark
Assistant Professor of English
University of Liberia
Monrovia

His Excellency Edward Martins
Ambassador of the Federal Republic
 of Nigeria to Liberia
Monrovia

Mary Antoinette Brown Sherman
President
University of Liberia
Monrovia

J. Teach Tarpeh
Vice President for Academic Affairs
University of Liberia
Monrovia

Stephen Yekeson
President
Cuttington University College
Suacoco, Liberia

Seminar Secretariat

Bertha Baker Azango, Coordinator
Associate Professor and Research
  Associate
Institute of Research
University of Liberia
Monrovia

Henrietta Badio
Secretary

Magdelene David, Coordinating
  Committee
Acting Institutional Research Officer
University of Liberia
Monrovia

Victoria Kennedy, Coordinating
  Committee
Administrative Assistant to the
  Vice President for Academic Affairs
University of Liberia
Monrovia

Rufus Pailey
Administrative Assistant
Division of Engineering
College of Science and Technology
University of Liberia
Monrovia

Henry T. F. Zayzay
Secretary

Contributors

Augustus F. Caine
Professor of Anthropology and
  Sociology
University of Liberia
Monrovia

Herschelle S. Challenor
UNESCO
Washington, D.C. 20006

Adelaide M. Cromwell
Director, Afro-American Studies
  Center
Boston University
Boston, MA 02215

E. U. Essien-Udom
Department of Political Science
University of Ibadan
Ibadan

Ruth Simms Hamilton
Department of Sociology
Michigan State University
201 Berkey Hall
East Lansing, MI 48823

Joseph E. Harris
Professor of History
Howard University
Washington, D.C. 20059

Willard R. Johnson
Professor of Political Science
Massachusetts Institute of Technology
Cambridge, MA 02139

Ali A. Mazrui
Professor of Political Science
University of Michigan
Ann Arbor, MI 48109

Davidson Nicol
Former Director
United Nations Center for Training
  and Research

Eustace Palmer
Professor of English
Fourah Bay College
University of Sierra Leone
Freetown

Pearl T. Robinson
Department of Political Science
Tufts University
Medford, MA 02155

Amos Sawyer
Dean, College of Social Sciences
  and Humanities
University of Liberia
Monrovia

Patrick L. N. Seyon
Vice President for Administration
University of Liberia
Monrovia

Elliott P. Skinner
Franz Boas Professor of Anthropology
Columbia University
New York, NY 10027

George Williams
Director of Investment Promotion
  Department
National Investment Commission
Monrovia

Index

Abbia, 102
Abeokuta, 54
Abolitionism, xiv, 15, 19, 128; African
  monarchs and, 58; course on history of,
  102; Great Britain and, 39, 45, 58, 128;
  humanitarianism and, 37, 39–40;
  United States and, xii, 58
Aboriginal populations, Liberian, 21–22,
  65, 69, 71–72, 76–78. *See also* Liberia;
  Subordinate majority
Academic freedom, 130
*Accelerated Development in Sub-Saharan
  Africa,* by the World Bank, 93
Adedeji, Adebayo, 10
Afghanistan, 35
Africa, Afro-American society and, 104–
  108; agriculture and, 38, 45–46, 80, 86–
  87, 109, 130; "Balkanization" of, xiv;
  Black churches and, 5–6, 25–28, 57, 99,
  128; capitalism and, 34–35, 51, 69, 139;
  climate of, 46, 60; cold war and, 16, 19;
  economy of, 10–12, 23, 35, 59–60, 80–
  81, 93–94, 97–98, 115–116, 130, 139;
  education in, xxi, 4–5, 11, 16, 28–29,
  57, 64, 71, 76–77, 102, 105, 108, 111,
  130–131; elite in, xiv, 20, 33, 43, 62–65,
  78, 129; emigration to, 15, 18–21, 27,
  40, 46, 58–59, 75–76, 105, 128–129;
  foreign aid to, 11, 80–88, 91–93; nation-
  states in, 16, 56, 68–69, 71–72, 105, 126,
  128; natural resources of, 34, 37, 45–49,
  128; politics in, xiii, xxi, 12–14, 44, 47–
  49; private investment in, 7–8, 11–12,
  60, 81, 92–93, 97, 126, 139; United States
  and, 120–122. *See also* African governments; African universities; individual
  African nations; individual European
  nations
"Africa and the Black Diaspora," 102
African (term), 117, 128
African/Afro-American Connection, the,
  xiv, xxi, 7; conferences and, 99–101,
  103–105; cultural kinship and, 9, 116;
  economics and, 11, 36–53, 55; English
  language and, 42, 45; Liberia and, 127;
  scholarship and, 99, 104-105; southern
  Africa and, 47
African-American (term), 56–57
African Association of London, 118
African Civilization Society, 20
"The African Cultural Presence in the
  Caribbean and in North and South
  America," 100–101

African Development Bank, 12
African Development Fund, 82, 86–88
"The African Experience in the Diaspora,"
  103
African Free Schools, 18, 117
African governments, diaspora studies
  and, 109, 110–112, 114; leadership in, 7;
  transnational corporations and, 60; uni-
  versities and, 107–108, 112, 114, 130.
  See also individual nations
African Institution in Britain, 18
African languages, indigenous, 15, 59,
  112, 140. *See also* individual languages
African literature. *See* Literature
African Lodge 459 of the Masons, 117
African Masons, 17
African Methodist Episcopal Church
  (AME), 18, 117; Africa and, 26–28;
  Great Britain, 27; Natal and, 28–29;
  South Africa and, 27–29
"African Personality," xiii. *See also* Négri-
  tude
African Protestant Episcopal Churches, 18
African students, in American colleges,
  11, 57, 102, 105, 108, 111
African studies, 99; African governments
  and, 112, 141
African universities, African governments
  and, 107–108, 112, 114, 130; African
  studies at, 108; Afro-American univer-
  sities and, 5; diaspora studies at, 100–
  102; liberal arts in, 109; role of, xxi-xxii,
  11, 119, 121, 124, 130
Africa Subcommittee (U.S. House of
  Representatives), 13
Africa Today, 113
Afrikaans language, 44
Afrikaners, 28, 41, 46, 68
Afro-American (term), 56–57
Afro-American history. *See* Diaspora
  studies
Afro-American studies. *See* Diaspora
  studies
Afro-Americans, Africa and, 22, 99, 104–
  108; black identity and, 9–10, 52, 106–
  107, 114; business and, 12, 55, 60; capitalism and, 36–37; contributions of, 54–
  55, 104; dependency and, 115–116; dis-
  Africanization of, 57, 128; education of,
  xiii, xxi; Liberia and, 22, 40–41; Pan-
  Africanism and, 42–43; politics and, xiii,
  13; unemployment and, 35; U.S. foreign
  policy and, 7, 13, 47–48, 139; world

149

Rockefeller Foundation, 111
Roosevelt, President Theodore, 25
Roots, by Alex Haley, 57
Rubber, Liberian, 75; commodity agree-
ments on, 86
Russwurm, John B., 19–20

Saint Helena, Equatorial Africa, 59
Saint Luke's Church, Washington, D.C., 54
San Pedro, 22
Santo Domingo, 100
Satellite technology, 7, 10
Sawyer, Amos, arrest of, 130; "Response,"
123–124
Scientific American, 79–80
Second African Diaspora Studies Insti-
tute, 101
Second-class citizenship, concept of, 63–64.
See also Dual citizenship
Second Development Decade, 79
Second General Conference of the UN
Industrial Development Organization
(UNIDO), 84
Self-reliance, 115–116; African economy
and, 9, 11, 98, 139; African governments
and, 123–124; definition of, 97; foreign
aid and, 139
Senegal, xxi, 38–39, 77
Senghor, Léopold Sédar, 44, 129
"Set-asides," 12
Settler groups, 63–65, 75–76. *See also*
Americo-Liberians
Settler states, 74–75
Seventh Special Session of the UN Gen-
eral Assembly, IFAD and, 90; U.S. aid
proposals and, 81–84, 91, 93
Seyon, Patrick L. N., 130; "Epilogue,"
127–131; "Summary and Recommenda-
tions," 125–126
Sharp, 58
Sheppard, Reverend William H., 24–26
Sherman, Dr. Mary Antoinette Brown,
xxi, 126–127, 130; "Foreword," xi–xv
Sierra Leone, colonization and, xii, 55;
Creoles in, 20; elites in, 72; English lan-
guage and, 42; Great Britain and, 129;
humanitarianism and, 40; identity crisis
in, 114; maroons and, 18, 58; repatriation
and, 15, 17–18, 40, 55, 58–59, 105, 128;
university in, 130
Silber, Dr. John R., xxii
Skinner, Elliott P., 32–33, 54, 127; "Personal
Networks and Institutional Linkages in
the Global System," 15–31
Slavery, agrarian revolution and, 39; capi-

talism and, 39; course on, 102–103, 108;
economic basis for, 33–35, 49, 127; Euro-
peans and, 16; Great Britain and, 41; his-
tory of, 57–58; impact of, 56, 115; Indus-
trial Revolution and, 38–39; Liberia and,
77; North America and, 17, 33; opposi-
tion to, 15–17, 24. *See also* Abolitionism;
Slave trade
Slave trade, 15, 24–26, 33–34, 38–39, 105;
Arabs and, 41; course on, 102; Great
Britain and, 41, 15; Portugal and, 16
Slocum, Clarence, 25
Smith, Gerrit, 58
Smith, Joseph, 20
Smyth, John Henry, Americo-Liberians
and, 21–22; American Negro Academy
and, 118
Socialism, 16
Socialist bloc, 140
Society for African Culture, xxi, 117
Somalia, 41
South Africa, Afrikaners in, 28, 41, 46, 68;
Afro-American missionaries in, 26–27,
128; apartheid in, 29, 47–48, 56, 129;
diamonds in, 46; Dutch language in, 44;
English language in, 44–45; Europeans
in, 16; Great Britain and, 28, 45, 68, 129;
host community and, 74; Nigeria and,
56; United States and, 48, 56, 60–61,
129; Western support for, 60–61; white
emigrants to, 46
South African Native National Congress, 29
South America, 33
Southern Africa, 46–48. *See also* South
Africa
South West Africa, 42
Sovereignty, national. *See* Nation-State
Soviet Union, 46, 60–61; Jews in, 48
Spain, colonies in Africa, 41; slavery and,
16; work schedules in, 60. *See also*
Spanish language
Spanish language, 59, 105
Special drawing rights (SDR), 83
Special preferences, policy of. *See*
General System of Preferences (GSP)
Spices, 38
SS Antonio Maceo, 49
SS Frederick Douglass, 49
SS Phillis Wheatley, 49
State, the. *See* Nation-State
Steel, trade agreements on, 90
Stockton, Calif., 57
Subordinate majority, 67, 71. *See also*
Aboriginal populations; Liberia
Sudan, the, 16, 39
Sugar, slavery and, 34, 38; trade agree-
ment on, 82, 86